Contents

Topic *Page*

Chapter 1 A New World

- Flying further than ever before 11
- A Different Town 13
- Cooking Thai Food Abroad 18
- The Scandinavia I know 20
- The In-Laws 21
- My first taste of Finn Food 23
- Getting a Caesarian 24
- Speaking Finnish 25

Chapter 2 Asking The Right Questions

- Safety 31
- Tik Ambulance 35
- Making adjustments 38
- Doing homework 39
- Woodwork 43
- Studying with the children 44
- School or factory? 45
- University education in Thailand 47
- TV Programs 48

Chapter 3 New Things In Life

- Life in Finland 51
- Inspiring designs 53
- Agriculture in Finland 55
- Moral Farmers 57
- Finn women, Finn men, and Thai men 59

Topic	Page
➔ Venting my frustrations	60
➔ Now let's talk about Finnish men	61
➔ Finn women's tastes	64
➔ Thai fashion	65
➔ Second family	68
➔ The long-awaited concert	69

Chapter 4 Back to Thailand for the Holidays

➔ Going home to Thailand	71
➔ My beloved brother	73
➔ What shall we eat today?	74
➔ My favourite concert	75
➔ The great illusion	76

Chapter 5 A Warm and Loving Family - The Greatest Reward

➔ Winning the lottery	83
➔ The gift that keeps on giving	84
➔ The grand prize, plus a bonus	85
➔ An economical vacation in Finland	86
➔ My confession	89
➔ Another Finn man that I love and the nickname "Golden Daughter-In-law"	90
➔ My beloved father	92
➔ The luckiest woman in the world	94
➔ My first son	95
➔ What to do after you graduate	98
➔ Skilled workmen	100
➔ A lesson for the ladies	103

| Topic | Page |

Chapter 6 The Star of Finland

- New social scene 109
- My second home, Caisa Cultural Center 110
- On the big stage in Finland 111
- Joining a choir with foreigners 113
- Singing Nawamin Maha Racha on television 114
- Our Vision Contest 114
- Not winning but being selected 115
- Culture 116

Chapter 7 Giving Back to My Motherland

- Chairwoman for the Finnish Thai Association 125
- A night honouring His Majesty in Helsinki 126
- The benefactors 127
- The Thai and foreign artists 128
- The attendees 130
- Loss is Profit 130
- Doing good 132
- An audience with the Crown Princess of Thailand 134
- Minister Counselor Siriporn Panupong 135
- On national television 137

Chapter 8 The Best of the Town

- As a Thai Chef 141
- My technique 142
- An old story 144
- Taste 146

Topic	Page
✈ Buffet food	147
✈ Giving thanks	148
✈ Setting up "Tamarind" Thai restaurant	149
✈ My own restaurant business	150
✈ Tired days	151
✈ My customers	153

Chapter 9 Happy Days

- ✈ My youth 157
- ✈ The willingness to learn 161
- ✈ My mother's inheritance 163
- ✈ Changing the reader 164
- ✈ 5 years of loneliness 166
- ✈ The music with fierce and aggressive beat 169
- ✈ Beauties in a fish tank 172

Chapter 10 12 Years in Finland and My Observation

- ✈ The other side of the coin 179
- ✈ Rights and equality in marriage 181
- ✈ Dao's story 183
- ✈ Great and meaningful books 186
- ✈ My English 188
- ✈ An open view to the world 189
- ✈ Compliment or insult? 190
- ✈ A development 191

| Topic | Page |

Chapter 11 My Lifelong Dream

- Looking forward and looking back 195
- Sightless 198
- Model Citizens 200
- Who to choose? What is the way out? 204
- Conflict causes change 204
- An Event for the Storybook 206
- Thai politics in the eyes of foreigners 207
- The following is a transcript of the section on Thailand in Lee Kuan Yew 208
- The caste system abroad 211
- Amazing Thailand 212
- Stepping past your fears 213
- Questionable work from the appointed government after the coup 215
- The light at the end of the tunnel 217

Chapter 12 Whose World Is it?

- A world without safety 221
- Black or white, we are all human 225

Acknowledgements 229
Praise for the author 230
Bibliography and references 237
About the Author 238

Foreword

I have never imagined that I would become an author today, just like I have never counted how many books I have read, since I was a young child up until the present day.

... *By a rough calculation, I would say I have read over a thousand books.*

This is the first time I have told my story in the most detailed and open way. I have taken old stories, dusted them off, and told them once again. It may offend some people, and I have been warned by well-wishers not to write stories that would bring harm upon myself. But I think that I have only one life, and this time, I am using this life to hold a pen and act as a medium to show Thai people things they have never seen and to help them relive things the things that they have seen before. I am proud to have the chance to do something I've always wanted to do, to choose the right side and make a bold statement that I am supporter of democracy. I have dug up some of the past that has been concealed, and I may be a catalyst to help Thai people who are unsure about the past take a backward glance to examine the new information that has come to light. I want to help them to come to their senses and be free from all the prejudice that the leaders of the past have convinced them was true. I also want to take this opportunity to tell you about my experiences, from past to present.

How did I get the nickname of **'Golden Daughter-in-law'?** That is another story that I want to share and tell from my experience. That is why I wrote about my life from the past to the present, so that you can understand why I have travelled so far away from home. That is why I want to tell you how I ended up on this road, which has been paved with emotion, from love, pity, sadness, anxiety, joy, gladness to so many other emotions, woven together to tell you my story.

Now, I have made a dream come true, thanks to my father (Pratuang Jitnarong), my mother (Preeya Jitnarong), my brother (Pachai Jitnarong), my sister (Pratana Jitnarong), my husband (Pasi Ilvesmäki) and Ratchaneeporn Phentrakul, who have supported and encouraged me on the way until this book could be completed. I sincerely hope that you will find this book entertaining, informative and useful.

Porntipa Ilvesmäki

Chapter 1
A New World

Flying further than ever before

I was about to get on the longest journey of my life. For nine to ten hours I would be sitting on board an airplane, flying me across the globe to another country on the other side of the world called **"Finland"**. Never in my wildest dreams had I imagined I would be starting a new life there.

As the plane took to the sky, my 9 year old son sitting beside me peered out of the airplane window, his face beaming with excitement. In my heart, fear was slowly starting to creep in. I started to miss my mother terribly.

My mother's sorrowful face flashed in the back of my mind. I recalled her expression as she heard the news that her beloved grandson and I would be leaving her, going to a far, far away land. She begged and pleaded with me to rethink my decision, complaining that the distance was too far : she would not be able to come and visit us. Who knows when we would meet again?

My mother's words never fail to bring tears to my eyes every time every time I think about her. She told me *"I don't really understand young love but more than anything, I want you to be happy. If it's what you want, and if leaving will make you happy, I will be happy for you."*

I consoled my mother and promised to take care of myself and my son to the best of my ability. I asked her not to worry. My husband, Pasi, also promised that he would love us and take care of us as well as possible.

It was the most important day of my life.

That day, I witnessed my mother's unbounded and unconditional love. She gave up her own hopes and desires so that I could be happy. A parent's love is the purest love, never asking for anything in return.

From then on, I loved and respected my mother even more. At the same time, I was saddened that I could not stay in Thailand to take care of her, even though my older sister was already doing this job wonderfully. To me, one of the duties of a good daughter is to be a pillar of support for your parents in old age. It is a job I would never be able to do completely, and this thought echoed in my mind constantly.

As the aircraft took to the sky, I looked out of the window to see rows of houses, as small as specks of dust on the landscape. I couldn't help but wonder, *"When am I going to be back to my homeland again? What does the future hold for us? What are we going to do in our new home on the other side of the world? Who knows?"*

I was lucky to be able to bring my son to live with me. Many mothers making the same journey have been forced to leave their children in Thailand due to not being fully ready to bring them along. I felt sorry for them. What torture it must be to be parted from your baby, to be so far apart. As a mother I could understand this pain only too well. I pulled my son close to me and whispered in his ear *"I promise, I'm going to take care of you the best way that I can."*

I was confident in my statement because at least I had perseverence on my side. To me, this word had magical powers. It would be my mantra, a spell to help us two get through any obstacles standing in my way.

A Different Town

The grey skies in front of my filled me with excitement and made me wonder whether the people in Thailand would see this shade of grey under the same sky.

Even with the summer approaching, cold gusts of blowing wind constantly had me pulling my winter coat tighter to me. The cold chilled my body and made me shiver, even though it was no longer the middle of winter. I wasn't used to this weather condition, so different from my country that I had left behind. I wondered if I would be able to make it through the winter.

In Finland, the whole city was spotless. The streets and sidewalks were clean and organised. The buildings, old and historical, looked mysterious and interesting, inviting you for a closer look. It is no surprise that Finland is one of the best places to live in the world. It is a world apart from the life I left behind, with the bustling streets and hurried people and the tropical heat that sent everyone into the icy old air-conditioning of the nearest department store.

The city I saw before me was not full of cars. The business district did not seem as hectic as Bangkok, which seemed much larger in comparison. Helsinki, the capital of Finland, did not have as many traffic jams or pedestrians as I had expected. I expected it to look like New York or San Francisco, with towering high rise buildings.

Pasi brought me and my son to his apartment, which was not too large. After we moved in, the place seemed to shrink considerably, but after rearranging a few pieces of furniture, it became very comfortable, cozy, and suitable for a small family like ours.

Even though the apartment was quite old, my son and I did not have to worry about anything. It was fully furnished with all the modern conveniences, despite them being quite old. The decorations and houseware were clearly over 50 years old but fully functional.

The next day, Pasi took me for a long walk around the city. It was not a huge sprawling metropolis as I expected and certainly paled in comparison to other large cities around Europe. There were no majestic castles like France or long shopping streets like Oxford Street in London, no frantic shoppers like the ones that cluttered the Champs Elysees of Paris, but the city was graceful in its simplicity and carried itself confidently with its own charm.

I was fairly clued in to world politics and had studied up on it a fair bit when I knew that I would be moving to Finland, so I knew that Helsinki is renowned for being the centre of political negotiations, earning it the nickname *"The Geneva of Northern Europe"*. Most recently, it was used to facilitate political negotiations between America and Russia. Finland is definitely a key player Europe, I thought.

It was hard to believe that despite the size of Helsinki, there were only nine hundred thousand to one million residents. This was less than some of the larger districts in Bangkok! Perhaps this was the reason that I felt cold all the time. Once the sun had set in the horizon, I felt a distinct loneliness set into my heart. Every time I looked up into the sky, I could not help but miss my family in Thailand.

... Were they looking up at the sky too?

... Was anyone missing us?

Pasi took me and my son walking along the street, with identical looking buildings. No matter where you looked, the buildings were similar to each other. He told me that this was because the city planning was a grid system, so different from my home town where the planning was a chaotic mess. Once you had gone down a soi, there was no hope of coming back to the same place you started. In Helsinki, there was no fear of getting lost. The reason that all the buildings looked similar is because of the Great Fire of 1808. Afterwards, the cityscape was planned and rebuilt by the Germans in a more organized fashion.

The winter nights were an especially lonely time. Most people preferred to stay inside to keep warm and only went out to go drinking during the weekend, and even those were mostly young couples or teenagers. Finland gave a lot of importance to conserving natural resources and campaigned to raise awareness inspiring their people to live frugally and not be extravagant.

On the contrary, in Thailand, there is hardly a place that does not keep all of its lights on, especially in official government places or even in private establishments. Every place keeps their lights sparkling bright, competing with each other for attention. In Bangkok, a mall's consumption of electricity could light up a whole village. Ironically, electricity is generated from dams, situated in the provinces, on farmland taken from local villagers to build the dams and to keep Bangkok lit and vibrant. Despite this, Bangkokians still waste electricity without a care or thought.

The contrast could not be clearer. I could see that Finland, which is highly developed, was enthusiastic about conserving energy and protecting the environment. I wondered if Thai people nowadays realize that a disaster is approaching. I only pray that my country could survive it and that no grave natural disasters would happen to Thailand, as I had seen happen to so many other countries.

Let's go back now to talk about an important city in Finland called *"Rovaniemi"*. Rovaniemi is a small town to the north of Finland. If Finland is shaped like a lady wearing a dress, this town would be situated on the left chest of the lady, which means that it is the heart of Finland. Situated just below the Arctic Circle, driving north for only 10 minutes you would reach Santa Claus's village, situated on the Arctic line. Above this line was the North Pole. The town is not too large: it is tranquil, with a lake and pine forest. The town is comprises of low-rise buildings and is surrounded by a body of water. In the winter, when the lake ices over a large number of tourists visit the town to take to the skis and snowmobiles. In March, the villagers take ice picks, dig through the ice to get to the lake underneath and go fishing.

There is also Lappland, where the local livelihood comes from dog farming and deer farming. The dogs are used for sledging. The villager's main income comes from tourism, but in the 6 months of winter chill, where the ground is white and the skies are grey, the locals manage to survive and wait for the next tourist season. How they do it is a pure mystery, I thought.

In Finland, transportation is very convenient. Even on the main roads, there is a designated lane left for the trams that run down the centre of the main roads. Buses, trams and trains work efficiently to get people from place to place.

I dreamed of such a convenient transportation system for Thailand, a system based on a solid foundation that is as efficient as those that can be found in leading cities in the world. My dream is coming true soon, with a government that represents the people, works for the people, and works for the common good of the people.

At the time of writing, the Thai government is planning and holding an exhibition about a development program that includes a mapping of a central transportation system and a high-speed transportation system that will transform the countryside, bringing prosperity to small provinces.

The new plan involves a mass transit system of 11 lines and a bullet train from Bangkok to other large provinces, which will also be interconnected by a motorway and 4-lane highway will be built all over the country. Most importantly, a deep sea port will be established in 3 provinces, Songkhla, Chumporn and Pakbara, with an industrial estate from Laem Chabang to Vietnam, as well as a gas pipeline through Burma, Thailand, Cambodia, Vietnam and Hong Kong. Thailand will be the centre of the ASEAN community. My family in Thailand will live a better life with better social services and a thriving economy. The benefits from taxes will be given back to the people in the form of the country's development.

I was overjoyed and prayed that these mega projects would be carried out to full completion. No more shaking by the sides of the road when you want to cross the road. Every time I do this in Thailand, I had to force myself not to think of the front page of the newspaper, where I would be the headline, a woman being run over while crossing the road. I am scared every time I cross the road at home.

I thought of Khun Paka's book, called *"Krua Hunsa, from Pla Ra to Wasabi"*, on page 44, where she mentions the landscape and cityscape of Japan; the roads which are friendlier to pedestrians and drivers who realize that roads are not just made for big cars. On the contrary, in Thailand while waiting to cross the road, she describes herself being transformed from a human into an invisible spirit standing by the road side, wondering *"which car is going to be the first to stop for me?"*

The last words were so funny I couldn't help but laugh. Soon, I thought, my country would be as developed as the one I'm in right now.

Cooking Thai Food Abroad

The smell of green curry hangs in the air and spread itself all around. The smell of Thai food is so strong that you can usually tell from standing in front of a building whether one of its occupants has a Thai wife. The thick aromatic broth of green curry, topped with little droplets of of oil and rich coconut cream when it reaches the right consistency, garnished with a few leaves of basil on top, is enough to send Pasi in an exquisite mood. He sits patiently, smiling at the corners of the mouth while he is thinking of the taste of what's to come. A little flattery from him will set into motion a full-blown Thai menu that would cost a small fortune in a restaurant, but I was a firm believer in flattery and Pasi never got tired of giving me compliments every day. It was enough to make me feel like an angel, but then I pinched myself I came and found myself back to the kitchen and was transformed into an ordinary kitchen slave.

The green curry would be accompanied by chicken and cashew nuts, which seems to be a foreigner's favourite menu. I could make chicken and cashew nuts with my eyes closed. At my restaurant in Thailand, Thais and foreign customers both loved this tasty dish, but I myself have reached a point where I do not even want to taste it.

My mother had a knockout recipe, which requires using your own homemade chilli paste. Take some dried chilles, garlic, shallots, and fry them together until they are nice and fragrant. Then, blend this mixture and cook again over a low heat. Season with salt, sugar and fry until the mixture turns dark. This makes a wonderful chilli paste that you can store and use whethenever you want. Making your own chilli paste will transform your food with a deep aroma and luscious colours, different from store-bought chilli paste, which is old by the time it reaches you, is less nutritious, and less tasty.

For chicken and cashew nuts, I take some pieces of chicken and lightly dust them with flour. Fry the pieces of chicken in very hot oil until they reach a nice golden colour and set them aside. Return the pan to the heat, fry up some garlic, followed by onions, paprika, water chestnuts, spring onions and baby corn. Season the mix with fish sauce, seasoning, tomato ketchup, chilli paste, and then add the chicken. Stir to mixture together, pour a little sesame oil over the top, top with some deep-fried cashew nuts on top, and the dish is complete.

The last dish to go on the table is a spicy and delicious tom yum goong, which also uses the chilli paste recipe. I will not describe the recipe in full detail here, as you, dear readers, may start to think you've bought a cookbook. When I turned around, I saw Pasi and my son grinning and waiting for the waitress to give serve them rice and water. I probably don't need to tell you that the waitress in our household is me. Every meal for dinner, there would be Thai food on the table, a tradition that has carried on until today. Even until now, Pasi still eats Thai food everyday without ever complaining. I can't believe that I travelled half way across the world to cook Thai food. It is quite easy to find Thai products. You can see all the Thai products as if you were in a market in Thailand - even the stone pestle and mortar, the seasonings, the Thai rice cooker, sticky rice steamer, or even Thai fruits and vegetables. The Thai Kitchen to The World program is probably a guarantee that, wherever there is Thai people, there is Thai food for sale, anywhere in the world.

Cooking Thai food abroad is all about adapting, since it is impossible to make everything as if you were at home. Whether you can compete with the high prices is another matter. Finding the equivalent or similar vegetables therefore can help you save a substantial amount of money without compromising on the taste too much. The fusion between Thai and Finn food is also another interesting matter, for example using Massaman Curry or Panang curry in Finnish pies. This was a hit with everyone and another item that can be easily added onto the menu. After this book, I think writing a recipe book of Thai and fusion Thai-Finn food would be a great idea.

The Scandinavia I know

When I was young, in geography and history lessons of Thailand and abroad, I would have to remember who the leader of the country was, what system of government they had and what their geography and culture are like.

The country leader that I have never forgotten until this very day is the First female prime minister of the world, Sri-Lankan Sirimavo Bandaranaike, and the second is Indira Gandhi of India.

Sirimavo Bandaranaike in particular was elected to be prime minister three times, and all as a result of elections, not revolutions or coups. I am especially proud that Thailand also has a female prime minister that did not come from a coup, the first female prime minister in Thailand's history, **Yingluck Shinawatra**.

When I was younger, the Scandinavian group of countries seemed far removed from my reality and I didn't really pay much attention in classes. I learned that Finland and Scandinavian countries are cold and snowy, and I was most familiar with Sweden, Norway and Denmark rather than Finland and Iceland. Sweden and Denmark have long established diplomatic relationships with Thailand, and the royal families have built close relations with the Chakri dynasty of Thailand.

Moreover, Sweden has a world-renowned band which is known all over the world, Abba, who won the Eurovision Song contest in 1974 with *"Waterloo"*. I have always loved Abba and when I started singing in 1974, I even used to sing a lot of their songs. I even performed their song, *"I Have a Dream"* on World Women's Day at the Caisa Cultural Center of Finland.

Norway was (and still is) spoken of as *"The Land of the Midnight Sun"* when actually, Finland also has a midnight sun, too. But I am quite sure that very few Thai people knew that back then.

Now, everyone knows that Finland is the producer of the popular Nokia mobile phones and the home nest of Angry Birds. I'm guessing that Finland is probably a name that is catching on more than other countries, just like Denmark is more familiar with Thai people because Thai-Denmark milk is a brand that is commonly consumed in Thailand.

The In-Laws

When **Pasi** said that he would take me to see his parents, my heart was beating fast with excitement. In Thai culture, the parents are the most important people in the family and thus, they have the utmost effect on the stability of your family. If they do not like the daughter-in-law, that could cause a very big challenge for the couple. Love and understanding in the family is so important that if there are any misunderstandings, the family could never be complete. In reality, the tension between mothers-in-law and daughters-in-law are a universal problem and could happen to any family of any race. The things you fight about only differ from culture to culture.

I had a Thai friend who could not get along with her Finnish mother-in-law. It was a troubling issue that was hard to resolve. Her mother-in-law did not want anyone in the family to marry someone of a different origin and refused to change her mind or be open to new things.

The daughter-in-law, on the other hand, had problems with adjusting. Coupled with the unwelcome treatment of her husband's family, the issue could only go from bad to worse and became impossible to resolve. The person stuck in the middle who could help to resolve the situation is the husband, but for some unfortunate women, the husband would often turn a blind eye when faced with the conflict, refusing to acknowledge anything at all. For those women, it was like facing double bad luck.

As the foreign in-law, if I was ever met with in-laws who looked down on Thai people, my family life would be full of unhappiness since I had no other family in Finland. My husband's family members were going to be my closest relatives. Looking back, If Pasi's parents had not been so nice to me, my marriage would be under a big, unhappy cloud of doom. But I was in luck: not only did his family not carry any prejudices, they welcomed me with open arms and treated me as if I was their own daughter. Pasi's parents are open-minded and modern. They are not quick to judge and do not base their opinions on a person's outside appearance. They were very kind to my son and I, living by the motto that whoever their son loves, they as parents would be prepared to love that person too.

I was so fortunate to meet them and my inclusion into their family was seamless.

My upbringing, with Thai customs and values, where the daughter-in-law has to respect her husband's parents as if they were her own, made it easy for me to adjust to them.

The longer time went on, the more I discovered that they were kind and generous people and the more I was determined to take care of them as well as possible. I wanted to make them proud of having a Thai daughter-in-law as a new member of the family.

My first taste of Finn Food

My life in Thailand was so full of happiness and being surrounded by good food. Thailand has delicious food from all different countries for you to try, especially in hotels and famous shopping malls. International buffets are so popular, featuring food from Italy, France, Germany, Korea, Japan, China, and much more. I was constantly on a tour to taste and sample them and hardly came back to eat at our restaurant, which annoyed my mother a lot. She often complained about it, but I explained to her that I didn't like eating at the restaurant because there is so much good food outside to choose from and it is hard to resist.

Just as people from other countries are wowed by the tastes of their own food cooked up by the international chefs of Thailand, when I got to taste the Finnish dishes cooked up by my mother-in-law, I found them to be very tasty and different from all the international dishes that I had tried.

Makaronilaatikko is a baked macaroni dish that everyone in Finland knows, especially the children. I was excited to try this new food and was pleased to learn that the preparation process was not that complicated. It can also be found in almost all the supermarkets in Finland at quite pocket-friendly prices.

Other dishes were just as tasty as makaronilaatikko. Pasi buys them for me quite often since I said I am bored of Thai food. Unlike me, Pasi is unwavering in his love of Thai food and could never be bored of eating Thai food every day.

Getting a Caesarian

I was scared of hospitals and usually refuse go near them. When the services of one became necessary, it was enough to give me nightmares. In this case, it was a hospital that I was not accustomed to and the doctors and nurses spoke a completely different language, which made it even worse.

As labour approached, the pain began to set in and my fingers got colder and colder. The nurses were trying everything to make me have a natural birth even though I had the evidence and papers that my firstborn was born by Caesarian section. Nevertheless, then nurses tried to convince me to have a natural birth, even though there was no sign of the baby coming out.

After 20 hours passed, I was ready to die. I looked at Pasi and tried to tell him to persuade the nurse to let me have a C-section because I could no longer stand the pain. I thought of my family in Thailand. What if I turned into Nang Nak Phra Kanong, a famous character from Thai folklore, who died during childbirth? Who would take care of my son? I realized I hadn't said goodbye to anyone in Thailand yet. I started to cry unashamedly and started to get angry at the nurse for not letting me have a C-section.

After more time passed, the doctor came to see me and probably saw that I would not make it. I was fast tracked to an operation in 15 minutes. I barely had any energy left, but tried to remain brave for my son and everyone around me. Pasi was with me during the C-section and was even paler than me, who was on the table. I had to laugh. He was probably scared that I was going to die. My condition then was so pathetic, so stressful, with the occasional wailing in between. Pasi held my hand and consoled me the whole time. The surgery went off without a hitch. I was overjoyed and grateful to the doctor for saving my life. During those long hours, it had occurred to me that I may have travelled all this way just to die abroad. What a shame that would be.

Even today, I am still terrified of getting a C-section despite all the competent doctors in Finland. I could not forget about the nurses trying to force me to have a natural birth.

Speaking Finnish

Learning Finnish was very useful for the future and for getting on with day-to-day life. Pasi's parents were most delighted because they wanted to communicate with me in Finnish rather than English. They can actually speak English very well, but their memory was fading since they didn't use English every day. The language caused a few problems in our communication as time grew on.

Finnish is not an easy language to learn, especially when not studying it as young, my memory is not as good as it used to be. Nevertheless, with a bit of hard work, it was not that difficult to master. I studied Finnish for about 3 months and then had to take leave to go back to Thailand for an audience with Princess Maha Chakkri Sirinthon. It was one of the most important moments in my life.

When I came back, I could hardly keep up with the rest of the class. I would sit at home crying, not knowing what to do. At the time, one of my friends, Wan, suggested that I could start working at a Thai-Chinese restaurant as a cook. I saw it as a good opportunity, getting work and earning a bit of money would also lessen Pasi's burden, without realizing that neglecting to study Finnish would make things more complicated and come back to haunt me in the long term.

Once I started working and getting a pay slip I was glad to be helping out my husband. Even until today, I work as a chef and I have never looked back at studying Finnish again. But this came to be the major source of problems and complications.

Firstly, I could not communicate with my children, whether it was teaching homework, or disciplining them and advising them in all sorts of motherly things.

Secondly, it made shopping at the grocery store very difficult. As a housewife, buying things for the home were a necessity, but often, I would buy things which could not be used or not what I wanted, since I couldn't read the label. Taking them back the next day was an unnecessary waste of time.

Another disadvantage is that I could not understand a lot of situations. For example, when there are announcements on the buses or in places I was at, I was as good as mute. Many times I would be sitting on the bus when the voice of the driver came on, after which people would start getting off the bus. I would follow them, even though I didn't know what was being said, and even today I do not know the reason I got off the bus. The worst disadvantage for a foreigner is the lack of opportunity to get a stable job : getting employment in Finland is no easy task because there are many Finns who are unemployed and companies would usually give them preference.

Foreigners seeking employment must be no less competent than Finnish people, and if they cannot speak the local language, their chances would greatly diminish. My knowledge about food helped me to get a job and make a living, but it involves communicating in Finnish to the staff at the restaurant also. Now, I can get by but I couldn't say that I understand everything. Luckily, I can practice on the job and could communicate with my children more and more as they grew up. As they started learning English at school, it helped to lessen the problem bit by bit.

Actually, it is not that hard for foreigners, especially Thai people, to get a job. During language classes you would get sent to work placements in various places and most would get employed because Asian people are hard working and generous. They do not complain about staying overtime to finish the job, and would be well-loved by their superiors. I would advise those who want to go and love abroad to learn the local language of those countries to create more opportunities for yourself

The Foreign In-Law สะใภ้ต่างแดน

Chapter 2
Asking The Right Questions

Safety

Everyone wants safety in their lives and to live in a safe environment. Lucky for me, Finland is one of the safest countries in the world. Wherever you go, there is no fear of burglaries, bag snatching, or if you want to leave your house to go somewhere for a long time, you don't have to be afraid of coming back to an empty home.

This safety seems like a blessing, and I was blessed with a much more beautiful and harmonious life than the one I left behind in Thailand, but deep down, I was not ecstatically happy. It's true that I had a great family, a loving husband, a good job and safe surroundings. It sounded like it would be enough to live the life that everyone wanted, but what was missing in Finland is colour and excitement. What makes me say that?

In everyday life, when you go to buy paint, there are many colours to choose from. You choose many colours to paint the most natural ambience, one that most closely resembles nature. One colour alone could not recreate that feeling. You have to use many colours to mix them and create new ones.

For me, living in Finland, I felt that Finland did not have all the colours to paint and complete the picture. Wherever you looked, there was black, white and grey. The lifestyle was repetitive and carried on the same way throughout the year.

I woke up to go to work in the morning, came back to cook at night, took care of the kids, watched TV and went to bed. I've been doing this for the last 12 years. Even if I went abroad on vacation, that only happens once a year. Why could I not have joy and colour in everyday life?

The entertainment TV programs in Finland feature interesting films from abroad and can help get rid of loneliness a little. Sometimes though, it can be annoying, with re-runs of the same old movies over and over, so often that I started to wonder if I had amnesia.

I saw movies like 007, Rambo, Spiderman and so many others so many times that I could play them in my sleep. Even the kids refused to watch it. Watching the variety shows, you get the sense that you've seen it somewhere else before. The only difference was that this was being replayed in Finnish.

Personally, if you asked me whether I found Finnish TV programs entertaining, I could not wholeheartedly say no. The entertainment programs are okay, but there were no programs that I had to watch every week, or wait for it to come on, not wanting to miss a single minute. I might be different from the Finns in that Finns like to follow the news and watch documentaries. Since the news cycle repeats itself time and time again during the day, they might get used to watching things that repeat themselves. Entertainment outside the home is even harder to find due to the cold weather and our friends lacking the time to talk or socialize all the time. Everyone had their duties to provide for themselves and to provide for their family back in Thailand. It was very rare to get the chance to stop and ask yourself, *"Am I having fun?"*

TV channels in Thailand have many selections to choose from and enjoy. Cable TV provides you with hundreds of channels, competing with each other to constantly create new ideas, as well as provide up-to-the-minute news, which is a bonus for the consumer seeking entertainment.

My mother cannot get around as much as she used to and sometimes has to be at home alone when everyone is out at work. Every time I call her, I can tell that she is enjoying a variety of TV shows and sometimes I can hear her laughter coming through the phone. She tells me that she is happy because there are so many things to watch on TV to keep her company, which puts my mind at ease.

Thank goodness for television executives in Thailand for helping entertain elderly people whose families are far away from them and making them less lonely. That is really important in the world we live in today.

Before I moved to Finland, my life in Thailand was fun and full of colour. I had time to go out, drink coffee with old friends, and feast at famous hotels, trying all their delicious dishes from around the world. In the evenings, we would cook up a storm and eat together in the family, sometimes swapping dishes with our neighbours. At night I would go out with my friends and listen to music at pubs and bars, there was a variety of jazz, blues, country, pop, disco etc. that you could listen to whenever you want.

As an ex-singer, I had a lot of friends and my life was never dull. There was always colour and entertainment. When there was a concert by a famous artist, we would have a get-together and have a great time. On the weekends, we would come up with excuses to head out to the beach, the waterfalls or the mountains.

Living in the land of snow, the chances to go out and do something as fun as before diminished. I had to take care of my family and kids. The weather was also a huge deterrent and the different environment made those good chances hard to come by again. Even with my Finnish neighbours, I could scarcely exchange a few words, like hello or goodbye. If I was closer to them, we would exchange a few questions and answers. Even now, I still can't find the kind of close friend that would go everywhere and anywhere with me. Everyone here has a lot of duties and obligations to fulfill.

I asked someone once how they felt about living in Finland, and they replied that they had to work outside the house, come back and cook for the family, take care of the kids, and the paycheck was quickly spent because of the high cost of living. Life continues in this way. I learned that it was not just me, but there were many other Finns who wanted colour in their life but did not have the choice.

I was not surprised to see that Thailand had an increasing amount of Finnish tourists every year. For me, who was used to the colourful life which suddenly disappeared, I was yearning for some reprieve. I longed for the day that I would be free of my obligations, whether it was work or taking care of the little ones. When they are older, I am determined to take Pasi home to Thailand, to go back to the life where we could go wherever we want whenever we want.

I believe that in our human lives, safety alone cannot make it complete. There needs to be the addition of colour and entertainment to keep us happy and stimulated. Why else would foreigners all over the world want to live in Thailand? At the moment, many nationalities worldwide can be found in Thailand, some of them even deciding to sell their house and home in order to settle in Thailand after their retirement. .

And what about me? A Thai person with a family and home in Thailand, who suddenly found myself in a cold and foreign land. If it hadn't been for love, I would have made my departure from Finland a long time ago. I could not even imagine how it must be for a Thai woman who was living here without the support of her husband's family, with an unsupportive husband. I could not imagine how terrible life would be for them. I don't know about other people living abroad, but for me, every breath that I took was filled with the hope that I could go back to living my colourful life like the good old days. I hoped that Pasi would be by my side experiencing all the fun and colour to reward him for all the hard work he had done his whole life. I wanted him to be happy and entertained by the local culture in Asia. Pasi, who loves to travel the world, would have such an amazing time with me as the tour guide, introducing him to the world of many colours once again.

Tik Ambulance

I had many friends who were restaurateurs in Helsinki. Even nowadays, we are as close as before. When I was new in town, I received invitations from all the partygoers to go and taste some new cocktails and have a change of environment. I didn't hesitate to accept the invitation.

When it comes to alcohol, I have tried all the brands available on the market, since my job as a singer required me to work in close proximity to all of those things. A few drinks before going on stage improved my vocals significantly.

Actually, that is a myth. I tried it before as a scientific experiment (but the scores didn't come out too well). The result was I forgot my lyrics. So, I was careful about drinking before or during a performance. However, after the performance I would make up for lost time, hardly remembering which drinks I'd had. With great company cheering you on, the musicians, the singer and the staff would party on until hardly any of us got any sleep. I would often wonder how we worked so many hours but yet nobody wanted to go home. It was much easier to pull up a chair and join the other night revelers for a few beverages after work.

Sometimes we would stay up until morning, have something for breakfast and make our separate ways home. Once, I was still living with my family, when I came home in the morning, my mother would ask me *"Did you go singing or did you go and sleep with someone, to come back this late?"* I did not reply but thought to myself that if I was sleeping with someone, I wouldn't be getting out of bed so early, I'd be coming home at midday or in the afternoon. But I didn't dare talk back to my mum that way, in case she had a heart attack, so I stayed quiet and listened to her preach at me, on and on, until I fell asleep.

My mother got angrier and angrier by the day until she gave me an ultimatum to quit my job and come back and help the family business. I couldn't do what she asked, since I loved singing and I loved the life of being surrounded by other fellow musicians. It made me feel challenged and I felt that my life was meaningful. I could stand on my own two feet and I earned a high salary that made me proud.

Back to Finland... after joining the crowd, the conversation was flowing freely. It was the first time I had gone out since moving to Finland, so I put on a good show. I drank whatever drink was handed to me without protesting. They passed me a black drink poured into a small shot glass which tasted like cough medicine you would find back at home. I didn't think it would be all that bad. This wasn't my first time.

Hours later I was in hell, hugging a toilet bowl. Then my world went black and the next thing I could hear was *"Can you hear me?"* It was the voice of the ambulance team, who had to revive me and nurse me until I became conscious. Before I knew it, Pasi was standing beside me with an amused smile. He probably thought I deserved it. Usually, when he poured me a drink at home I would often refuse, saying I don't like drinking. But this definitely proved otherwise.

I used to boast to Pasi that I could drink all night and a day, which he saw for himself when we first met. He liked the fact that he had found someone he could have a few drinks with. In Finland, however, I hardly wanted to drink. It wasn't that I was trying to be good or anything, but when I was younger I think I had taken enough alcohol into my blood stream so when I got older, something happened and my body didn't want to handle it anymore.

Pasi brought me home after carrying me off the ambulance. When I opened my eyes again, it was late afternoon the next day. As I recollected last night's events, I leapt out of bed in a panic, wondering how I got home. Pasi made me something to eat with my eldest taking care of me not far away. My eyes welled up with tears, feeling sorry for my family that had to serve me. How could I not know how much I could handle? I probably forgot that I wasn't as young as I used to be. I apologized to Pasi and promised never to let it happen again, and I have never done that since.

Nevertheless, the name Ambulance Tik was imprinted in everyone's memory. In Finland, there are many Tiks, so whenever anyone wanted to make a reference to me, Ambulance Tik was the clearest way to get the message across. How could anyone forget? Even Pasi joined in : if we were going anywhere and an ambulance was passing by, even at the slightest sound of the sirens, he would say *"They've come to pick you up!"* It was our inside joke, which made the children wonder why he said such a thing. I didn't dare tell them the truth and had to explain that daddy is kidding, and then we would exchange a knowing look. When we got home, he would pour me a glass of wine, for his drinking companion.

I learned what it is like to drink with good company. Drinking for happiness and pleasure with someone you love is much more enjoyable and much better than getting drunk.

Making adjustments

No matter where you are, being able to adjust is the best form of self defense you can have. My new country was so different from the country I left behind, whether you're talking about the weather, the culture, the religion or even the way people live.

Going out to work required the aid of the bus, train or tram. Sometimes, I'd have to use all three before getting to my place of work. Fortunately, the transportation system is modern and punctual, so that you can do everything correctly and on time, and the best part of all is that there is no traffic.

The only thing that was a major inconvenience is the absolutely freezing weather. The roads were covered in snow, which made it difficult to walk. I had to be careful of every step for fear of falling down. A broken leg would be a real setback to my plan to travel the world.

The other frustrating thing was that people were not that smiling and didn't really pay attention to each other. Everyone went their own separate way, which dampened my smile also. I hardly got to smile during the day. When I got home, I wanted to smile but the mass of plates and dishes piled up into a tower made me rethink it before taking over my assigned role of kitchen slave. I had to perfect this role of the perfect Thai woman, wife and mother no matter what. Secretly I thought to myself that King Rama V abolished slavery in Thailand, but slavery seems to have popped up in foreign kitchens worldwide instead.

I'm not just talking about Thai women, but this statement also applies to women all over the world who are slaves to their husbands and children, dedicating themselves and never getting a chance to look at themselves and be slaves to their own dreams.

We do not know how much time we have left in this life. Personally, for me, I've taken a look at myself and I'm living my dream, trying to fulfill my own goals. Life is yours, you must be your own master.

Doing homework

Helping the kids with homework is nothing strange for the normal family, but it is strange for me. Why? Since I spoke a different language to my children, how could I teach them homework? When I taught the children elementary math, which had numbers, that was quite easy. The kids were confused as to why I was so good at adding, subtracting, multiplying. Before that, they must have suspected that mummy never went to school.

Maths was an easy subject for me. When I was in school, I liked to add and subtract while I waited for my dad to pick me up, and I can recite the timetables off by heart even today. Not to say that I was top of my class in math, but I did reasonably well. I didn't like the class much because the teacher never paid attention to us, so I could talk to my friends or doze off in class. Sometimes, my friends and I would skip math class to meet up with friends from other school, who came by to pick us up in their fancy cars.

We liked to head to the beach in Songkhla and go to the movies, until we got caught and got sent back to school. We were punished by shaming in front of the flag in the morning and spanked with bamboo sticks 10 times each, as well as a letter getting sent to our family. My luck couldn't have gotten worse: I unexpectedly ran into my parents at the cinema. They had also run away from the kids to watch the same movie.

My double bad luck was that after the public spanking in front of the flagpole at school, I was also spanked by my mother until I thought I would catch a terrible fever from it. I cried myself to sleep, hoping for some sympathy from my brother that never materialized. My teacher wrote a letter to my parents, which I was not allowed to carry home because they were scared that I would destroy it before it found its way to my parents' hands. I didn't dare tell my teacher that my parents already knew that I had skipped school from running into me at the cinema. The next day when my parents were invited in for a meeting, the whole school found out about what happened. I never so much as ventured near the gates of the school during school hours again. I also paid more attention in Maths class.

Let's go back to talking about me teaching my children homework. After teaching them Maths for a while, the kids became less impressed when the tasks started to contain Finnish questions. I didn't understand what they meant and I didn't dare to teach the kids, in case the teacher calls me up to yell at me for teaching the wrong things. The kids didn't ask me to help me with homework ever again, which hurt me a bit as they were probably wondering why I couldn't read and speak Finnish, or, simply put, *"Why is mummy so stupid?"*

Things eventually became less stressful when my children started to learn English, so we could communicate better, and I could resume my teaching duties. This, however, came to a halt soon because as I have gotten older, my memory has became quite bad. Most importantly, the schooling system in Thailand and Finland were different. I did not want to confuse the kids, so I thought it best to stop my tutoring sessions.

When I was in middle school, all the scores of every subject were averaged out, for example, if you were not good at Math but good at other subjects, you could pass the grade overall. However, when I entered high school, the Ministry of Education changed the grading system to individual grades, which got me nervous. My studies was taking longer and becoming more stressful. I was scared I would not pass. I didn't like subjects which required calculating, like Chemistry, Math and Geometry but when it came to reading, handicrafts or anything that involved memorizing, nobody was better at it than me. I loved to read and memorize and can still recall subjects like History, Geography, and many others today.

As Maths exams approached, I bought the friend that was good at this subject offerings of sweets and snacks every day, as well as flowers for my beautiful but strict teacher. The guys liked her because she had beautiful legs. Her face was okay to look at, but she had such beautiful legs and would wear skirts that cut off above the knee to come and teach every day. Even I couldn't resist having a look. I gave her flowers often, and she smiled and thanked me until I was sure that I would get good grades. It was the last year of high school and if I got good grades, it would count a lot towards going on to further education.

I made plans with my friend to sit together on exam day, thinking I would get good grades because my friend was great at Maths. When the results came out, she got an A but I got a C. I immediately approached Ms. Nice Legs and asked her why I got a C. The answer was *"All of your answers were correct, but I gave you a C because you copied your friend. I took pity on you because you have a kind heart, but you are lucky you didn't get a D."* I was mortified. Skipping school and not paying attention in class was finally coming back to haunt me.

Copying was a terrible offense that could get you disqualified from taking the next day's exams. Ms. Nice Legs, however, was kind enough to let me take the next tests. I guess the flowers worked. My friend who let me copy from her got a caution from the teacher and was told that she would be disqualified if it happened again. I was scared to do it since and couldn't even look at my friend's face during exams. My not paying attention to studies was not only harming me, but my kind and gentle friend also had to suffer because of it. Nowadays, my friend is a professor at a university. She is not yet married, and whenever I go back home, we always meet up to reminisce about old times.

Speaking of this particular friend, her life revolves around books and studies that never end. I have had long talks with her about books, and every time we meet she would bring me good books to read, and I would bring my good reads for her also. Her books are literature and political history, which she knows I am interested in. I bring her books on love, food, fashion, DIY and handicrafts, which she does not really pay attention to. I then understood why she is not yet married.

My favourite writer is Kampaka, who I introduced to my friend. Now she has more books by Kampaka than me, and it seems like she is changing herself from wearing thick glasses to contact lenses and adding a little more colour to her wardrobe. She has started to wear makeup and started wearing a little glossy lipstick, just like Kampaka.

I was glad to hear that she has started going out with someone, a professor in the same university. I was as excited as if it was my own boyfriend, both feeling excited and hopeful for her. I hoped that she would always be happy and open herself up from her former life where she was closed to the idea of love and having fun.

I regretted on her behalf some of the time that she let pass until there is so little of it left, but it wasn't too late for her to start changing her mind and herself. I saw the sparkle and hopefulness in her eyes and thought how different it is from 5 years ago, when they were so dry and hopeless, when she was stuck in her own ways and her own thoughts and not being open to new things, even though I tried to suggest them all the time. After she read Kampaka's books, my friend changed into a different person.

... Thank you Khun Kampaka, my favourite author.

Woodwork

While studying in Thailand I had the chance to study many handicraft subjects, whether sculpting, carving, dying, fabric painting and many other arts that I love, but my favourite subject had to be woodwork, which seemed more suitable for guys. I was really good at it and always got full marks. When I showed by mother, she asked me whether I picked up somebody else's grades by accident because she couldn't believe it either (which made me quite upset).

My mother was mostly too busy with the family business to know what I did at school, but my father knew everything. He was supportive and encouraging. When I moved to Finland, I didn't think that I would have any use for this subject ever again. One day, I saw my 9 year old daughter busily sawing a piece of wood with her three friends. When I enquired, she said that they were making wooden swords like the movies, so I volunteered to help.

The entire group of children turned around at the same time with disbelieving looks in their faces. Personally, I could never walk away from a challenge and I got busy finding new wood and a new saw. I drew a lion's head on the handle, inspired by the logo of the Finnish police, and polished up the work with sandpaper. The children couldn't believe their eyes. Pasi walked around with a smile playing on the corner of his mouth, not volunteering to help and mocking my skills at the same time.

The children took their swords to show their friends, who all wanted me to make them one too. Now I was in trouble. My arm nearly fell off from just making one because the wood was so hard. I didn't want to say no, though, because I didn't want to hurt their feelings, so I told them that I would make them one if I had some free time. They have probably forgotten, but if any day they remember, I would have a long list of orders to fill out still.

Pasi was probably amused and thought I deserved it for boasting and volunteering. But one day if I ever had to make a whole bunch of swords, you can probably guess who I will be forcing to help me out.

Studying with the children

Even though I had studied under the Ministry of Education syllabus in Thailand, which is a formula with a considerable amount of standards, when I got the chance to study with my children in school and started following up on what they were learning, I found that what I had learned was so outdated, and the teaching in European countries is so modern and world-class.

This is not to say that Thailand's schooling doesn't have its standards: Thailand has won gold medals in all sorts of academic competitions. That is proof that Thai children's IQ is not lower than other countries' at all, but Europe has to be commended for making their teaching easy for the children to understand.

Finnish education is amongst the top in the world. What I like most about it is there is no private tutoring necessary outside of school. They separate kids with different IQ's into different groups and there are two teachers teaching the same subject simultaneously but in different rooms. That enables the teachers to better prepare kids who are not as quick to learn as their peers. At the end of the class, the class joins up together again. Those who have questions don't have to be intimidated by their smarter friends. They are free to ask the teachers whatever they want and the teachers cooperate fully.

I feel tired for parents who have kids in the Thai education system. Some of them build up heavy debts in order to send their kids to school, hire a tutor, or send them to expensive tutoring schools after class, including Saturdays and Sundays. The children hardly have any time to themselves or to do other activities with their family and friends. Thai children spend more time studying than any other country, but they do not perform better. Why? Because Thai studies place emphasis on the old way of learning, reciting things like parrots. The children have to work hard to memorize a ton of books.

In France, there is a movement to stop teachers from assigning homework to students. The classes must be finished in the classroom so that when the children return home, they have a chance to spend time with their families or to play together to rest their brains.

In Thailand, children have to complete their homework during their tutoring sessions, even though sometimes the tutors at tutoring school are the same ones as the ones that teach in the school. I don't understand why teachers can't just explain or teach everything that is required in the class. They keep something held back so that the kids have to continue studying after school, and the parents have to pay the expensive tuition fee after school for them to do so. Adding up school fees, tuition fees, school lunches and snacks after school, it is a wonder that parents don't go bankrupt sending their kids to school. Some have to go into debt so that their children have a bright future with good jobs. The parents have to struggle to send their kids to school without ever knowing if they will get to see the fruits of their children's success.

Nowadays, there are many Thai people abroad who have to work hard to pay the horrendous tuition fees for their children staying in Thailand, including paying for tuition fees on top of that. The divisions in Thai society creates competitiveness in schools and universities, with many parents competing to send their children to famous and expensive schools and universities where the school feels are supposed to indicate the quality of their knowledge. This is the sad fact.

School or factory?

It is nice to see some high school students from Thailand coming out to make a proposal to the Ministry of Education to change the education system and offer a more equal footing for kids with different social statuses to attend the same school.

Another important part of the proposal mentions the competition between each school. Every school competes with each other to get the most representation of their students in entrance exam results, which will bring fame to the school and make everyone want to attend that school.

One member of the group who submitted the proposal to the Ministry of Education admitted that teachers would tell their students to study hard for the school's reputation without considering how much pressure they are putting on the students. The students have to compete to make the school famous. In the old days, schools were a place where kids and the youth were developed, but nowadays, the school is more like a factory, where kids are put through the factory, ranked to compete with each other, before they are put on the market.

Another important observation is that the style of teaching is still very scientific, with based on just memorizing. In every exam there is only one answer and if the student answers differently than the teacher, that means that they are wrong. In reality, questions can be answered and interpreted in many ways. If a student has a different opinion than the teacher, if does not always mean that the student is wrong.

Moreover, the students proposed some changes from the outside and developing the curriculum by themselves. One of the subjects which really must be revised is History, which Thailand needs to consider the facts which they can bring to light, or English, which has to comply with international standards. The English curriculum used in Thailand is written by Thai people and cannot compete with other countries which use an international curriculum. That is why Thai youths who graduate from university still cannot understand 100% of the international curriculum.

I watched these youths in the media and felt glad that Thai youths are starting to come together to develop the system of education in Thailand to newer heights. They were brave to represent millions of other children in Thailand who were too afraid to stand up for fear of being expelled from school. I admired them greatly and hope that they can move Thailand forward, with Thai youths standing at the centre of the nation's future development.

University education in Thailand

Thai society places a lot of importance on having a university degree. It is giving importance to what's on the outside, with the general belief that university graduates must be ethical and moral creatures, held up in as high regard as the degree that they hold. This makes Thai society ignorant to learning outside of the academic system, which is to say, libraries, operas, theatre, museums, industries, handicrafts, technology, and most importantly, other cultures.

This type of informal education is the kind that can be accessed by anyone, whether they are market vendors, taxi drivers, blue collar workers, or even prostitutes. Anyone can broaden their horizons and take a look at what is going on in the world outside Thailand, outside of the immediate country that they are living in.

Technology has taken us a long way where you can find knowledge anytime of the day, anywhere. It's now not necessary to be studying for a university degree in order to discover knowledge for yourself. Having a degree is good and important to having a good livelihood but it doesn't mean that people without degrees are incompetent, less moral or less ethical, and they certainly don't deserve to be mistreated.

Nowadays, Thailand has a generation of modern, forward thinking people. Everyone has awareness and knowledge, even in the provinces. Even people living small towns have had the opportunity to study using modern technology in a way that would surprise urbanites, who still think that villagers are stupid and ignorant.

For instance, **Dr. Thaksin Shinawatra**, Thailand's 23rd Prime Minister delivered a populist policy for people who live outside the social security system, especially the 30 Baht Health Care Scheme, which has caused significant changes in the villages. Holding frequent local elections has also made people in remote villages come to see that their vote is valuable.

It comes as no surprise that, whereas before, Bangkokians and people who live in large cities dictate who wins the elections, now, villagers are the ones that select the government. As a former villager, I am delighted and proud of their progressive thinking, and their awareness to be involved in politics and not remain passive towards politics any longer.

TV Programs

The cold weather on weekends makes us hesitant to go out anywhere. There is also a strong desire to rest the body that has to work 5 days a week, for several hours a day, without getting to sit down apart from during lunchtime. I turned on the TV and I was greeted with something that put me in a bad mood, which was a TV show with dishes from several countries around the world.

One of the segments of the show was about making Thai food, which had me frowning as the famous chef demonstrated making Thai food using the wrong ingredients and doing things in the wrong order until I could hardly stand it. I turned to tell Pasi to vent my frustration, which only increased as the program went on. Pasi could only sit there and move his eyes from side to side, not knowing what to do.

I was very familiar with Thai food since I worked as a chef, with a lifetime experience of cooking behind me, since my family owned a restaurant and I graduated in Food and Nutrition. I was so saddened and couldn't understand how someone could use their fame to ruin the recipe of a dish that they weren't familiar with, destroying the nutritional value and taste of a dish that is not their local dish. They should be shamed! As well as that, it showed a disregard for the millions of viewers who took notes and got the wrong recipe to make that dish. It made me doubt the originality of the other dishes that were being demonstrated on that show.

I loved to watch cooking shows more than anything and loved to make those dishes whichever country they were from. When I saw that cooking show, I didn't want to follow the other recipes that were being shown. The only way to learn how to cook is to learn from the native chefs of that country. Since we're on the topic of TV shows, I would like to vent about a few of my frustrations. I saw American TV shows and admired their professionalism, creativity and originality. The entire world is entertained by their game shows and many other countless shows that I could watch day in, day out. The only thing that annoyed me is the show that pretended to be original, but is not. I felt so bad and couldn't accept it. The only thing I could do was turn off the TV. I reconsidered the words of those who claim to hate America, however, a lot of shows from the US are copied all over the world. People may claim to hate America but their behavior is hypocritical.

There are other TV shows that I love to watch in Finland. I love the documentaries, world news, and sports. All day, you can have hours of interrupted pleasure with little interruption from advertising, unlike Thailand. Nowadays, there is more freedom in the press and I especially admire the programs that present a different viewpoint from the norm. Thai thinking in the past has always repeated the same thoughts we were taught with, so much so that Thai people don't know how to think for themselves. Only a few people dare to present revolutionary ideas that benefit the society.

At the moment, Thailand really needs to have factual news and TV stations that dare to expose the truth without being afraid. Public opinion that is being expressed on SMS's sent from home and shown on TV are another step forward towards freely expressing one's opinions.

20 years ago, Thailand was in the group of democratic countries all over the world, but now, Thailand is excluded from that group and has been likened with China, North Korea and Somalia. Therefore, if Thai television can present the facts that no one has ever dared to present before, that means that Thailand is becoming a democracy again.

What's sad is there are a number of Thai journalists who have stood by and let a military government make them turn a blind eye. What's even sadder is that they've watched fellow journalists get their rights stripped back without doing anything. Worse still, there are some foreign journalists who have received money from certain interest groups to attack the rightfully elected government, which has made the situation go from bad to worse. That's why I am glad that there is media and television stations that have stood up against the coup and those who have benefited from the country for a very long time. That way, Thailand can have a real and fully-fledged democracy.

Chapter 3
New Things In Life

Life in Finland

As a foreigner in Finland, my life is not exactly a life of luxury, although not a life of hardship either. The heart of it was about being diligent and patient. For those who have not worked hard before, it could be hard to work in a job that uses a lot of hard labour.

The first time I worked as a chef in a restaurant was quite brutal. Fortunately, I only had to season the food, invent the menu, take stock and order goods. There was a Chinese sous-chef that helped to do prep and that took a lot of the burden off me. The only unavoidable problem was having to stand the whole time and only being able to sit down when you eat.

When I first moved to Finland I was enthusiastic about finding my own income to help relieve my husband's burden. I had many ideas about making handicrafts to sell during summer, such as Thai dresses for barbies, artificial flowers, carved soaps, etc.

In the summer, everyone came out for a walk in the sunshine and people set up tables to sell goods at various places. The trading spirit was fun and I met a lot of new friends who were fellow vendors. A lot of them had great jobs but liked to come out and earn extra income during the weekends. The vendors would talk amongst each other and in the evening, we would support each other's businesses if there were things that went unsold. Sometimes, we exchanged goods, and often I would come home with great cheap suits, perfume or makeup at great prices.

Above everything else, I came home with pride that I could use whatever I had learnt as a child to earn extra income abroad. It's a wonder that when I was in Thailand, I never had the chance to use this knowledge for business, partly because Thailand was so flooded with these types of handicrafts that were readily available. However, being able to use this knowledge for my own benefit in Finland made me realize that having extra knowledge never goes to waste. In the future, you never know when it will come in handy, especially living so far away from home.

Inspiring designs

When I had the honor of participating in a question and answer session on World Women's Day on 8 March 2012, there was one question in particular that I wanted to answer, and that was the question, *"How do you feel about the Designs of Finland?"*

I must admit that the first time I saw Marimekko, the famous Finnish brand's designs, I was not that impressed. Maybe it was because I wasn't familiar with those patterns. Personally, I preferred intricate patterns like Thai silk since those patterns are more distinct. Wherever you take them, most people can tell straight away that the product is from Thailand.

However, after I saw the Finnish designs more and more, my feelings started to change. I started to see the individuality in the designs and some symbolisms that say something about Finland. Even when popular fashion has changed over the years, the individuality is still reflected in the pieces. Whenever I see designs in the style of Marimekko, I instantly recognize that it is Finnish design.

Nowadays, Marimekko is a brand that is famous all over the world. Even in Thailand, celebrities, models, and socialites love this brand. Even I couldn't resist and splashed out on a few pieces myself. Whenever I go back to Thailand I simply have to buy some as gifts, which makes everyone so happy. I bought it once for a television presenter and ended up on-air showing off the brand, telling the viewers about beautiful and good-quality designs that can't be bought in Thailand.

Personally, I think Marimekko clothes are more suitable for Asian climates, but unfortunately Marimekko is not on sale in Thailand. Thai people who love this brand have to fly out to Japan, where it is very popular, to get their fix of Marimekko.

However, when I asked other Finns, I got the reply that they don't like this brand, saying *"I don't think it's very pretty"* (maybe that's just one person). I think it's normal for people in the country not to like their own brands, just like Thai people love brand names from abroad while foreigners love Thai silk and Thai batik prints.

Taste is a freedom that should not be controlled. Anyone of any race can like beautiful goods from other countries. Everyone has the right to aspire to what they like and we don't need to be too patriotic about these things.

Agriculture in Finland

While driving up to the north of Finland, you can see agricultural products being grown. Potatoes, wheat, corn, strawberries, and many other agricultural products are grown in rows visually pleasing to the eye. It reminded me of the rice paddies at home. The livelihood of these farmers are very good. They have a modern lifestyle and have time for themselves and their families.

I have a Thai friend who married a farmer and have heard her recount the stories. It was then that I came to realize why the life of Finnish farmers is so happy and enviable.

Firstly, Finnish farmers have absolute power over their industries and are protected from entrepreneurs. They can control the price of fertilizer, pesticides, seeds, and can determine their own prices.

Secondly, they have bargaining power in the free market and are protected by the laws.

Thirdly, they have all the necessary tools and machinery, imported from other European countries.

There is a reduction on import tax for their tools and they can order them at affordable prices. Put simply, they are truly capable of enhancing their production capacity. You often see Finnish farmers sipping wine and watching the stock market to study the prices of their agricultural products on the Internet.

This was modern agriculture, highlighting that this career is another business career. Finnish people think that being a farmer is no different to owning a bank, owning a restaurant or a piece of real estate. They do not think that farmers are beneath them.

In Thailand, the farming profession is seen as inferior and not highly valued because of their poverty and debt. The land ownership, taxation and monopolistic hold over the industry by a couple of interest groups controlling the price of fertilizer, pesticides and seeds leaves farmers little room to bargain in the market.

Most importantly, there are no tax breaks on tools and machinery, which are imported from abroad, leading farmers to have huge debts. They have to borrow a lot of money to buy the expensive machinery. To make matters worse, fertilizer, pesticides and seeds are expensive because of a monopoly on them raising prices constantly. Those farmers do not have a choice and are not supported to get the right information about what to grow and how much of it to grow in each year. If they had this information, they could find other supplementary income in other businesses to help them during the year.

The farmers need a place to borrow investment with low interest rates and a stronger co-op system. They need access to technology to increase their production capacity. Hardly any agricultural products from Thailand are regarded as premium in the supermarkets of the world. Even the vegetables that are exported to Europe are often found to contain too much pesticide and have to be thrown out at the airport.

I used to think that Thailand was so full of natural resources and that farmers are helped by the government. On the contrary, a fashion capital like France is said to be one of the most fertile countries in the world. In Thailand, capitalists can buy a whole mountain to build mansions, hotels and private roads whereas villagers who farm on that land are thrown in jail. The classic story of the farmer being cheated by middle man has been going on since before I was born, and it makes Thai people not want to be farmers.

I am delighted that Yingluck Shinawatra's government sees the importance and value of Thai farmers, especially rice farmers. They have spent a great deal on research and provided support in science and technology. Most importantly, the government has helped with financing from the Bank for Agriculture and Agricultural Cooperatives, taking care of access to the world market and alleviating debts for farmers. I hope to see the smiles of farmers, not just photoshopped pictures on postcards that tell the story of happy farmers like we used to know. In reality, farmers have been oppressed by middle men and mistreated from government agencies for such a long time. I hope that with the support of government agencies and the new government, farmers can be treated fairly and have a better livelihood.

Moral Farmers

I read an article on the website of **"Kon Kin Kao"** network to support farmers, in which they declared their mission to maintain the dignity of farmers and to produce organic, pesticide-free rice which is good for the earth and its ecosystem, to grow rice for the good of humanity and to raise the level of moral awareness and ethics of farmers. They wrote that even though farmers grow organic rice, if they cannot develop their inner self and if they allow themselves be controlled by vices such as drinking, smoking, gambling, consumerism and immoral behaviour, farmers will never be able to escape the trappings of their current lives and will remain in debt, losing their land and their inheritance for the future generations.

This is the brief summary of the full article, which I could not bear to write in full. When I read the whole message, I was worried that I might throw up my dinner. I did not understand these people - who do they think they are, to preach or criticize and assume that the poverty of farmers is the direct result of alcoholism, gambling, consumerism or an immoral lifestyle. To look down on the support system of the nation without producing any evidence to support their claim is shameful. I don't know how noble they think they are themselves. Those farmers have the right and the freedom to do earn a living with their own conscience without needing anyone to pity them and to guide them, thinking that they are superior to others.

The middle and upper class, who the farmers produce rice for, have a producer-consumer relationship with the farmers. No one has the right to tell the producer how to live their lives in order to get rice that is full of morals and ethics. It is a vile concept and I think that whether farmers use the money that they earned to buy a car, a mobile phone, or to install a satellite dish, or whether they choose to spend it on alcohol, gambling or cock fighting, it is entirely within their rights. The upper class does not have the right to take away their freedoms. Each has to respect each other's rights. They cannot say that they want to support the farmers because they want the farmers to be noble citizens for the society in order to grow rice that is ethical and moral. The writers of that insane article should go back and think how much rice they've consumed since they were kids. If farmers did not have enough morals and ethics to grow rice in the past, those people would not be around today. When farmers grow rice, they want to create a good crop that can get a good price, too. Whether the consumer chooses to buy rotten rice, white rice, black rice, smelly rice or fragrant rice, that is entirely up to them in order to apply pressure to the producer. They do not need to pretend to the support the farmers while trying to control their lifestyle. Whether farmers want to raise their children to be doctors, prostitutes or beggars, it is their own business. Their downfall does not come from the lack of adopting the attitude of sufficiency living or living an immoral existence. Rather, it comes from the structure of business, society, corruption in politics, and laws that passed through all the checks and balances of government which has resulted in stopping the distribution of wealth from the upper class to the grassroots farmers. What farmers need is for the government to see the value in their profession and to help them by providing low interest loans, debt relief, marketing and giving them information about exporting and applying pressure on the middlemen to give farmers fairer prices.

That is to say, the article, written by someone who claims to be a knowledgable person with a doctorate degree, who claims to be a good person, should ask themselves how much soul and morals they have. Just because they think that they have knowledge and work in an air-conditioned office does not give them to write an article like that. They have no right to shamelessly try to control the lives of others, especially because they come from a different social class and status from the farmers. They should try rice farming for a day to know that farming with morals and ethics is like. As someone who has relatives who are farmers and have been raised by those who Thai people call the spine of the nation, I declare these upper class writers.

Finn women, Finn men, and Thai men

The picture that I see in the parks of Finland are the scene of a Finn woman holding a small toddler's hand while pushing a stroller with a baby inside while the little one hangs on to the side of the stroller.

Even when Pasi and I take the train with our family to go and visit his parents, I often see Finnish women looking after their husband and active little children. I secretly commended them for performing their housewife duties perfectly.

In Thailand, it is easy to find a nanny, and without a nanny one could ask the relatives of the family to take care of the children. In Finland, however, married women have to take care of their family by themselves and it is very unlikely that relatives will come to help out, as they have their own duties to take care of as well.

I asked a lot of Finn women who were married to foreigners, especially the ones married to Thai husbands, what the men are like. The answer that I got is that Thai men are gentle, romantic, hardworking and good cooks. I thought that fate is a cruel joker.

When I was in Thailand, I was never lucky enough to meet the dreamy man that they are talking about. Instead, I met a Finn gentleman who had travelled all the way around the globe until fate lended a hand and helped us to meet each other.

Talking to my husband's friend's wives, I discovered that Finnish women are smart, gentle, and very respectful towards foreigners. I felt at ease when we met up for the first time. Even 13 years on, this has not changed. Before coming to Finland, I was under the illusion that European women must be sassy and stuck up, but my experience taught me that they are a lot more polite than I thought.

In particular, Pasi's two sisters' mannerisms and words tell, that they are two ladies who have been taught extremely well by their families. They respect and love me and care for me as a sister and always give me great advice and a warm welcome, treating me like one of the family. I also love and respect them as if they were my real sisters.

Venting my frustrations

When I was invited by a women's group to speak about Finnish women from the view of a foreigner, I had to tell them that I was most frustrated about this topic. It was hard to be critical about what might be true. Maybe it was because I had a lot of Finnish friends who were all different in their own way.

If I had to be critical I would say that ....

... I like Finnish women because they are responsible to their family and their jobs.

...I like Finnish female ministers and senators, who are strong and proud.

...I like Finnish women who are eager to learn, modern and open to the world.

...I like Finnish women because they are kind to foreigners and not prejudicial.

There is a lot to like, now let's talk about the things that I don't like.

...I don't like some of the Finnish women who are not open-minded, look down on foreigners and openly display their prejudice. Sometimes they call you out to your face without manners.

... I don't like some of the Finnish women who take advantage of foreign labor at work and talk about them openly, thinking that they are not able to understand.

... I don't like some of the Finnish store attendants who looked at me like I couldn't afford what they were selling or like I was trying to steal it.

I think I'll stop there. Otherwise I might get deported sooner than I think... My opinions are probably just one viewpoint based on my own experience. That is why it is hard to tell the truth, but sometimes, it is good to express your opinions anyway.

Now let's talk about Finnish men

From my experience of Finnish men in my encounter, especially the one closest to me, Pasi, I can say that Finnish men are not the normal girl's ideal of being romantic or a smooth talker. On the contrary, Finnish men are quiet, keep to themselves and like their solitude. Sometimes could you meet one for a few hours and he will only say 3-4 words.

My friends who have gone out with Finn men have often said *"Why are Finn men so cold and boring?"* When I asked what cold and boring means, they explained that even though they tried to carry on the conversation, they only got half-hearted replies.

I thought that the reason the men acted that way was because they want to be polite and tried to be careful, since they did not know whether the girl had a boyfriend or not.

Personally, I liked the gentlemanliness of Finnish men. They do not care much for clubs, since they like their personal space. Whenever foreign women go anywhere in Finland, you don't have to be scared of being harassed, because Finn men don't like to approach strangers.

Especially Pasi, there is nothing to worry about at all even when he travels abroad for work since he doesn't really like to talk to strangers unless it is absolutely necessary.

Once, this was a problem that did not work in our favour at all. Since Pasi doesn't really pay attention to anyone. Sometimes when we pass by each other, he keeps his head down and carries on without even seeing me. I have to be the one to greet him first, much to my frustration. When we went to Italy a few years ago, I followed him around as we looked for our hotel, dragging my feet in my high heels. He refused to stop and ask strangers for directions. Finally, I had had enough and couldn't walk anymore. I went over to ask an Italian man who was passing by, and, as it turns out, our hotel was just a little way away and he volunteered to send us to our hotel.

On our next trip abroad, I was very well prepared with a backpack, trainers, and lunch for eating along the way because I understood that Pasi doesn't like to ask strangers. If I didn't respect this, then we would be grumpy with each other, so I'd rather adjust to fit with his personality. Then, I was ready to travel with him feeling at ease and happy.

Pasi's friends are also absolute gentlemen and love their family one hundred percent. I might write about selfish Finnish men who are abusive to their spouses, but I have never met anyone who is like that who are my husband's friends. On the contrary, I have been lucky to meet so many wonderful gentlemen like Pasi, his father and his friends. I want to share my experience about a very impressive Finnish man : Pasi's brother-in-law.

I met Pasi's brother-in-law, Olavi Lappalainen 13 years ago. At first, I was surprised to see a European man cooking, looking after the kids, cleaning the house as well as balancing a job as a high-school teacher. His wife had a job as a doctor. Therefore, a lot of the important duties around the home fell to the husband. Not only that, he was kind and gentle to his mother, taking care of her at all times, and handling the funeral arrangements when she passed away. I was touched by the love from a son, expressed to his mother through the music that played on that day. I cried with tears at the sad music which spoke of the sadness for the departed.

As I sat in the car on the way back from the funeral, the image of a man playing the cello was still stuck in the back of my mind and I can still remember it to this day. It made me realize there are so many good men left in this world and, depending on your luck, you will meet one sooner or later. I was lucky to have met mine and there are many other Thai women who are lucky like me too.

I guess the next topic has to be mentioned, and that is, the topic of Thai men. In my opinion, Thai men are romantic, sweet talkers, eager to please, and the biggest bonus of all is that they will cheat on you. No woman can stand it. That is how problems in the relationship regularly occur.

Nowadays, it is strange for a man not to cheat. It is a fashion amongst Thai men to have second wives and mistresses. All of these euphemisms sound mysterious and interesting and makes the men sound less bad in the eyes of society.

At the same time, the fact that Thai men are players makes them so charming. They are so skilled in talking and making women believe them. After a few sweet words and 500 excuses, women will easily agree to be taken advantage of once they have fallen under the guy's spell.

I have seen some women agree to let their husband have a new wife and live under the same roof, even let their kids play together. Sometimes I don't know whose baby is whose, since they share the same father and look so alike. That is a special skill of Thai men; European men do not stand a chance of competing.

Thai women are so used to this behavior from Thai men, but there are millions of them who are fortunate and have found faithful, responsible Thai husbands. At least my mother and sister are some of them. I may have been unlucky not to find a good Thai man, but I was doubly lucky to find a wonderful Finnish man. I thank the heavens for making us meet despite the distance.

Finn women's tastes

I love the way Finn women dress during the summer. In that time, you will see beautiful, colorful clothes reflecting the various fashions, be it the bags, clothes or shoes. All of them are colorful and express the national happiness for surviving half a year of miserable weather. The girls will dress up stylishly in tank tops, sporting backpacks filled beverages and hop on their bicycles to go and relax in the park, lakes, or rivers that are dotted all over the country. Some wear tiny bikinis and lay out to enjoy the sun. I would be interested to wear bikinis like them too, I thought, if I had their bodies and sexiness.

This kind of atmosphere only exists in the summer time. During winter people are covered up until you cannot see what they are wearing inside. If I wanted to keep up with the fashion, I could only look at it from the magazines. In general, I think that Finn women have a simple taste and don't dress too extravagantly, unless it is for a really important ceremony. Most of the colors are a muted tone like black, grey or brown. The colourful clothes only make an appearance during the summer.

Fashion shows are actually a frequent occurrence and there are many shops that sell clothes and famous brands. Finn women can follow the trends quite easily but from what I noticed, they do not run to keep up with fashion or do not dress to compete with each other. Most people live simple lives and do not like to go to social galas. Their social calendar consists of graduations, weddings and birthdays.

Finnish women usually dressed trendy and classy and focused on the materials more than the fashion of the item. It is a reflection of the remarkable frugal culture in Finland, which I am quickly picking up: I like the sophisticated look, but the pieces must be versatile enough to be used on many occasions too.

Thai fashion

I think Finns would have to surrender to Thai women when it comes to fashion. Like many societies in Asia, Thailand also has a tendency to judge each other from the outside.

So, Thai guys and girls pay particular attention to the way they dress, especially those who are well-off, well-paid or business owners. They usually wear expensive clothes and expensive jewellery to show off their better social status. That's why Thailand is full of shopping malls selling imported brand-names. Ladies with middle income or, as we call them, office ladies, put up a good fight with fake copies of brand names that are readily available on sale.

They can dress up and follow the latest fashion trends at an affordable price. Clothes designed by Thai designers are beautiful, with nice designs. Some of them are exported for sale abroad, generating billions of baht. Prominent Thai designers abroad include the likes of **Thakoon Panichkul**, who has a very famous client, the First Lady of the United States, Michelle Obama.

When I was in Thailand I was also in the fashion business and I'm very familiar with designing of the clothes because I took a dressmaking course before, therefore I have no problems when it comes to dressing and can usually mix and match expensive with inexpensive things. For example, I could wear a brand name matched with discounted trousers. When I moved to Finland, I focused more on saving and would wait for the sales to come in order to buy high-quality but inexpensive goods.

I think Thai women are more fortunate than others in that Thailand has beautiful and cheap clothes ready to buy, and many shops and department stores offering them. Therefore Thai women developed the habit of loving clothes and naturally loving to dress up.

That is just a few things on the tastes of normal women, but there is another breed of women out there: actors and high-society. You can see those women at the Oscars, the Thai Suppanahong Awards and other award ceremonies. At the end of these events, the fashion critics would come out to rate the best and worst dressed, along with their reasons. I love to read this, admiring the nice clothes as well as learning about fashion, social etiquette and the latest trends according to each fashion designer.

Of course, it has to be said that the Thai entertainment industry cannot compare to Hollywood's. I feel sorry for Thai actors who have to pay out of their own pocket for their hair and makeup, and then walk around in the awards to get talked about by the journalists or gossip queens in society. Due to the limited funds, their overall image tends to come out wrong.

I don't think those actors are on top of the trends and know all about fashion. If you got anyone with an ordinary job to dress up for the awards, you would have to worry about they dressed. Even the pretty starlets with nice faces and bodies can hardly pull it off. For us ordinary people, going out at social functions with not such pretty faces and bodies can sometimes be very tough. Before going out to a social event, I would circle the mirror feeling distressed, hardly able to look at myself and face the image in the mirror.

What has happened seems to have stemmed from a lack of cultural knowledge in terms of dressing yourself. Western culture and influences has intervened until people are confused. They don't understand why you can't wear flats to an evening event, why they cannot wear flip flips with office attire, why they can't wear rainbow colours after thirty, or why they shouldn't wear short skirts to get on the bus or off a boat. It looks all wrong.

If I ever see a heavily made-up woman, with a coif bigger than her face, eyebrows drawn so thick it looks like it was done with a marker, you don't have to tell me for me to know that she is a high-society Thai person. The bright red lipstick that is all the rage in Thailand is so intense and heavy that it seems like the wearer is a vampire waiting to sink her teeth into the next victim.

In Europe, using bright red lipstick can brighten up the dark skies, and wearing colourful clothes can fill a fog-ridden atmosphere with freshness and enthusiasm. In my opinion, paying attention to the way you dress is quite important.

I have a friend who loves the natural look. She does not dress up and thinks that putting on makeup is nonsense and a waste of time. Whenever I meet up with this friend, I hardly want to talk to her, since the woman that I see is hardly a woman I would want to look at twice. Which man would want to look at her? The image that greets me is a woman with tousled hair, who has never been to a facial treatment in her life, with nails that have never seen a nail file, let alone nail polish. There was no foundation on her skin and dry lips without a touch of lipstick. It made me kind of mad. How can she love herself so little? Women who know how to dress and do it well are smart women. They know the society, know the world, know others and know themselves. I would urge all women to consider this. At the very least, if it does not cheer up everyone around you, do it for yourself.

Second family

When I first moved to Finland I did not have even a single friend, so Pasi took me to socialize with his best friend's family. That is Raija's family. I actually met her when I met Pasi in Singapore for the first time. I felt that she was a very gentle and friendly person. When Pasi invited me to go and visit them, I immediately said yes. She gave us a warm welcome and I am so happy that we made friends with her.

After that, whenever I went to perform, Raija's family usually came along to give me moral support, which made me very grateful and deeply touched. To this day, we love each other like family and I feel that apart from Pasi's family, I have another family by my side. During seasons and festivals, we usually meet up to socialize and I'm able to exchange conversation and opinions with her, especially on motherhood, in which we encourage each other. Because of her family, my foreign life is no longer lonely. At least I have a close Finnish friend who is like family to me.

The long-awaited concert

When I came to live in Finland, I had the chance to attend many concerts by world-class artists like Madonna, Whitney Houston, Britney Spears, etc. My now 22 year-old son and I love the same kind of music, so we never missed an opportunity to go to the concerts of famous artists that we loved.

When I was a teenager, I used to sneak off to discotheques and dance the night away until it closed. Now that I'm 52, I hardly thought that I would have the energy to move my legs along to the music for hours and hours like when I was much younger.

But as soon as I walk into a real live concert and hear the voice of my favorite artist, I would be possessed by a dancer's spirit that made me sing and dance along just like all the teenagers until the concert ended. Even though I would be thoroughly exhausted at the end, I felt that it was fun and worth the torture. Pasi was very understanding of this and fully supported me by buying me the concert tickets every time.

One day, the concert of my dreams arrived. It was a performance by a tribute group for Abba, organized at the Savoy Teatteri on 30th March 2012. As a die-hard fan of Abba, there was no way I was going to miss this concert. The performance was a performance of Abba music through Mamma Mia! as well as many other performances of their favourite hits. I couldn't believe that this group could portray the character of Abba music so well and so impressively. I felt as though I was watching a real Abba concert.

I was so overjoyed to be watching that concert. It seems that I was the only Thai woman in the crowd. A Finnish woman came up to me during intermission to ask me whether I knew Abba, so I told her all the great things about them as well as the history of Abba. She seemed really pleased and said that she couldn't believe a Thai woman like me could be such a true Abba fan like her.

If I had still been in Thailand, I wouldn't have had the chance to watch a good concert by such great artists because of the high prices of the tickets. My dreams were able to come true because I was in Finland. I was especially grateful to be in this country that gave me the chance to watch a concert by my most favourite band, Abba.

Chapter 4
Back to Thailand for the Holidays

Going home to Thailand

I was so overjoyed to be going back home. I counted down the days until it happened. I missed my mother, my relatives and wanted to see my home country after 2 years of being in Finland.

I missed my home in Thailand every day. There was not a single day that I didn't think of home : when I had to walk in the cold to get to work, when I took the bus home alone every day after work, or even when I got home and cooked for my children and husband, I missed Thailand even more.

Living abroad, I could honestly say that I have never worked this hard in my life. I felt defeated and wanted to go home many times, but the love and kindness from Pasi and his family put that thought out of my head. Most importantly, my love for Pasi made things change for the better, and made it easier to bear the cold.

When the plane touched down, I didn't realize that I had started to cry. I never dreamed or imagined that I would have the chance to come back. I went to greet my mother who cried and lamented about her woes of waiting for me to come home. My brother and sister were relieved to see me again and my sister told me that while I was abroad, my mother spoke of me every day and no one really knew whether I was doing well and how Pasi was treating me. When I heard this, I could not hold back my tears. They did not know that I thought of them every day and my life was not as glamorous as they might imagine. My life was not transformed like the princesses in fairy tales. But I couldn't tell my family that living abroad was not like living in heaven. It was not even close to that, but everyone has to live with their decisions once they have made their choices.

Finland taught me to be a new person: to be patient, wise, to think for myself, to be responsible, to give for others. Maybe it was the environment and the people around me that inspired me to change for the better, and the fact that I had made a promise to myself that I would fight for my children and family.

My family in Thailand was celebrating seeing each other again, which was a culture shock for Pasi. In the Thai custom, treating each other to a meal is a display of the love and care you have for one another. My brother told me to order whatever I wanted to eat, so I complied by ordering everything I wanted to eat in Thailand. In Finnish culture, they would never be so reckless in ordering food. It was more normal to eat until you are full and not more, but I was unstoppable. Pasi could only sit and blink. The hot temperature did not make him sweat as much as seeing me order more than 15 dishes on the table. I felt sorry for Pasi for witnessing Thai eating culture for the first time.

I thought my family was relatively normal. If Pasi had got to meet a rich family, he would have fainted for sure. I think he is still lucky to have only witnessed my family ordering food - the burden of paying belonged to my family in Thailand, as it was customary to take care of out-of-towners who had come to visit. My mother, sister, brother and other relatives took turns to treat us.

If Pasi had been the one paying for it, he would have fainted and never woken up again. This is only the first introduction of many other interesting scenarios. To be continued...

My beloved brother

There is a song by a Thai singer called **Rawiwan Jinda** called *Pee Chai Tee San Dee*, or My Good Brother. The lyrics, which speaks of a brother taking care of his sister and encouraging her when she is down, telling her not to be afraid of the world, always reminds me of my own brother. The love and care that she has shown towards me fills me with gratitude towards my brother, who has always been like a father and a friend.

During our misfortune at losing our father so suddenly, I was always fortunate to have my brother by my side. Even though I grew up and had my own family, he never stopped caring for me, in fact, it only seems to have made him care more for me.

I remember that before I came to Finland, my brother's final words to Pasi was *"Take care of my sister well. If one day you don't love her any more, please don't hurt her. Just send her back home."* His love for me is so great that I never felt like my father was gone.

What shall we eat today?

While in Thailand, I was taken care of very well, especially when it came to eating. The most common question was *"What do you want to eat today?"* which made me feel that there was so much joy to be found in choosing a good place to eat and delicious dishes of the day. Wherever I wanted to go, my brother would willingly drive me to all those places, and most importantly, pay for everything. Whenever I saw him pay, I started to feel bad. I tried to sneak off and pay, but my brother would never let me.

I guess it was a good thing that Pasi knew that my family never thought of taking his money or interfering in this matter at all. Every time we visited Thailand, the duty to pay would fall to my family: if we went to my mother's, my mother would be the host. If we stayed over at my sister's, it would be her duty to take care of both the accommodation and the meal.

The person who took on the burden of collecting us and sending us to the airport, sending us to meals and being my bodyguard, watching my every move, is my beloved brother.

My brother and I have always been close since we were kids. We grew up and went through everything together. We would help each other out when helping our parents with chores. We also shared similar tastes in music, food and political views. We also both loved to cook, as well as sharing many other passions. My brother and I could talk about everything, even personal matters.

In my life, I have often made my brother concerned and upset, since I was a stubborn person and sometimes made my mother cry. My brother would have to console and encourage my parents, which made me feel guilty, but he was never upset with me and never said anything to hurt my feelings. Whenever I was sad and needed help, he would lend a helping hand without ever saying no.

I was so proud of my loving and caring family. They took such good care of me and my children and never abandoned us. Their love for me never faded and I felt so lucky to have such great parents and my brother and sister in my life.

My favourite concert

Every time I came back to Thailand, I wouldn't miss the opportunity to watch my favourite concerts. I tried to select the dates which best coincided with the concerts, and I could easily go and watch whichever ones I wanted since my brother worked in this business.

One of my favourite bands is **The Impossible**, an old group that has been forever in my heart. I could hardly believe that The Impossible have performed in Finland twice before at the Crown Hotel, between 4-28 September 1974 and 1-31 September 1975.

I once took a song from The Impossible, *"Chao Phraya"*, and rearranged it for the choir in Finland . They were all excited by the beautiful melody as I translated the lyrics and told them about this famous band, who are still idols in Thai people's hearts today.

As I watched the concert, I was transported back to the past, to a time when I was listening to those songs with my brother in the house. My brother was an adoring fan and transferred his craze to my sister and I, who were influenced by his taste in music.

When I was a teenager, our family was selling food. Everyone was so busy that we couldn't watch television, so we'd put on the radio. At that time The Impossible were the most popular band that was being played by all the stations, several times a day. The three of us were absorbed by their music and remembered every word.

I couldn't believe that 10 years on, I would have the chance to see one of my favourite bands in concert once again. It was like a dream come true. I had my brother to thank for organizing this great gift. It made for such a special and meaningful time while I was visiting home.

The great illusion

Most of, or you could say 80% of Thai women who live abroad prepare a large sum of money for visiting home. Of course one had to give money to the parents, which is an important part of Thai tradition, to show respect and gratitude to your parents by taking care of them when they are old.

Although it might seem that returning home every time is a costly experience, with most of the money being spent on family, relatives and friends, it is a source of pride and joy to the giver, all of us living and working abroad. Most of the money came from our sweat and tears, but we are happy to give it away until there is none left. As it is, the day before getting on the plane to come back again, we would have spent everything until we hardly have any money left.

That is the spirit shown by Thai women who live abroad in tough conditions. Some people get manicures and get their hair done before going home; they find nice clothes to wear and take their family and relatives out to fancy places to show them that they have had a good and comfortable life abroad.

Perhaps that is why people think that Thai women who get married and live abroad are comfortable and everybody wants that life. But in reality, the truth is not as it seems. It is all just a great illusion. Those women still have to work hard when they get back. The glossy polish on their nails quickly disappears. Moreover, some have to work extra to pay off the debt they borrowed for going back to Thailand

Life abroad is hardly the fairy tale it seems. In actual fact, it is a lot harder than Thailand. Some people who have never scrubbed a toilet before have had to do it for the first time here. If not, they wouldn't have the money to spend on themselves or their family back home.

If you're expecting your husband to provide for you and wait on you hand and foot, you'd have to wait for the next lifetime. Before marriage, they would find you anything you wanted, but some couples barely make it to a year before getting divorced.

Some foreigners put on a great show when they go to Thailand. They dress well, take care of the ladies however much the bill might come to and buy them things. The women think: This is it! I can depend on this person forever and decide to leave home. When they actually get here, they have a shock because the home is tiny and dirty. They can no longer get whatever they want to because the husband is stingy.

The husband in Thailand and the one in Finland is so different, like being in heaven and hell. But, once you are here, what can you do? Those women have to put up with it to wait for their relatives who are trying to help them at home. Let's not mention the husbands, some of them are even unemployed, it is so pitiful. So the lesson here is, do not think moving abroad is such an easy thing. Think carefully before moving, or you may end up as a maid in a restaurant or worse, a toilet cleaner.

The illusions that we put on are really important to Thai people living abroad. They want to reassure their family to not worry about them. As well as this, spending an extravagant amount of money brings a source of pleasure to those who can hardly afford to do that in Finland. Therefore, spending back in Thailand is a source of pleasure for those who have the chance to go back home, like a type of release. I don't see it as a negative. As long as Thai people are hardworking, we can always survive.

78 The Foreign In-Law ละ-เมียงแคน

80 The Foreign In-Law สะใภ้ต่างแดน

Chapter 5
A warm and loving family

Winning the lottery

The age old saying that once observed *"Finding a good husband is like winning the lottery"* corresponds to my real life events so well, because I learned that finding a good husband is as hard as finding a needle in a haystack.

It might sound pessimistic, but from my past experiences until now, whether through things that I experienced myself or heard from my friends and social circle, it seems that most women suffer most from failing to make it as a couple.

A lot of them have good jobs, good social status and beautiful faces but end up getting disappointed in their marriage. I also had my heart broken in my first marriage and I could have never dreamed that I would find such an amazing husband today.

The gift that keeps on giving

My gift that keeps on giving is the fact that my husband is a careful, frugal man and doesn't spend unnecessarily. Pasi grew up in a family that likes to save. His parents are the typical Finnish couple who live modestly and simply. Even though they have good financial status and a comfortable life, they do not spend money frivolously, and don't buy extravagant things. They only buy what is necessary and things that can be used for a long time. Pasi also developed this habit and has been very careful with spending since he was a child.

I admire this habit a lot. Pasi does not go to parties unless it is completely necessary, he doesn't drink and party with friends and doesn't buy clothes for himself. However, when it comes to spending on the family, Pasi never says no. He is a real gentleman who is truly responsible to his family.

When I was younger, my family in Thailand also told me to be frugal with spending, but I never paid attention to their advice as I was too busy listening to myself. When I saw the example of my Finnish husband and the sacrifices he made for the family, my opinion quickly changed.

Now I realize that as a housewife, I should help Pasi save up in as many areas as I can, so that we can have savings to spend when it is really necessary.

I feel that having a husband who is the model of saving is really a gift that keeps on giving. With him, I am confident that I will never be poor and never end up penniless. If I take his principles on saving, my family will only flourish and not flounder.

The grand prize, plus a bonus

Winning the lottery is a great thing unto itself, but when it comes with a bonus attached, you could say that you really hit the jackpot. This bonus is having a husband who is like a father and a friend, and moreover, Pasi really understands me, as if he is inside my heart and mind.

When a famous magazine in Finland, Kauneus ja Terveys, requested an interview with me in April 2011, there were approximately 16 questions, all relating to culture and my personal life.

I spent a lot of time preparing the answers only to find that Pasi had already answered all of the questions and was waiting to send the information to the magazine. He was only waiting to ask my opinion on whether I was satisfied with the answers he wrote.

I was annoyed that Pasi didn't ask for my opinions first and beat me to answering the questions. It was only after I calmed down and found time to sit down and read what he had written, as he requested, that I found myself totally in the wrong.

The details that Pasi had written out were all correct, factual and accurate reflections of me. You could say it was even better than if I had answered them myself. The language he used was beautifully written and to-the-point. I found myself regretting getting angry and making a scene without considering all the facts first.

In that second, I realized what a valuable thing I had, finding a husband who knows me and understands every detail about my being, showing how much he has cared about me all along. On the contrary, I didn't understand him very well and often got angry at him for no reason. Pasi never held this against me and was always willing to help whenever I needed him. Regardless of what subject matter, he never said no and was always more than happy to support me.

Now I realize that I won first place in the lottery and also got a bonus because Pasi is so amazing and so understanding of the person that I am.

I made a promise to myself to always take care of him, in return for my great prize. The heavens are not always so kind in this way to all women. When I received this great blessing, I will do my best to protect it.

An economical vacation in Finland

I used to stress out about vacations because we would have to set aside a huge amount of money, and then come back from vacation to work really hard to make up for what we spent on vacation.

After that, our family had a new strategy: we would vacation at Pasi's parents' house instead of going far away. Their house was in the north of Finland in a beautiful surroundings close to the lake.

This sort of vacation helped us save costs because we saved on spending on accommodation, as well as being attended to by Pasi's parents. Sometimes we would even get a small amount of money as a parting gift! Vacationing in this way, Pasi could relax totally, without worrying that I would spend too much money shopping. I could relax and lounge about the house. Even though I had to set aside some time to look after Pasi's parents, I didn't have to work all day.

I loved the atmosphere of the old house. It is a single storey house that was built around 1962. The interior is very well-maintained, with 3 bedrooms, one living room, a sauna room and a kitchen.

The walls of the house are adorned with photographs of brothers, sisters and relatives of Pasi's parents, as well as pictures of him and his sister from their childhood. As well as this, there are paintings from Pasi's mother on the walls, making it almost impossible to find a free space.

The interior design tells the story of a house in long years in service. The wardrobe and the drawers are full of things. I loved the way the bedsheets are organized, rolled up to about 12 inches each and then separated by colour, as if we were in a department store and they were items for sale.

One room in the house that I loved in particular is the room that used to belong to Pasi. This room contains bookshelves and toys, like an old model toy car made of iron and plastic, as well as crafts made my Pasi's sister, showing how well Finland taught handicraft and design to their youngsters. From what I could see, their ability for handicraft is not bad at all.

Another favourite room of mine is the kitchen, which is equipped with anything you could want in a kitchen, tidily sorted and stored away. When on vacation there, I usually prepare a lot of Thai ingredients to bring with me, ready to cook Thai food for everyone, focusing on mild and tasty but not too spicy food for the whole family to enjoy.

I loved the equipment in the kitchen. Some of them are antiques dating back 70 to 100 years, but still in very good condition. My mood changes with the equipment that I use. When I work as a chef in Helsinki, I am in a modern and convenient kitchen with a slicer, dicer and deep fat dryer. Everything was designed to work efficiently, as one of the leading and modern restaurants in Europe might be.

But when on vacation, I had to use old equipment and utensils, and they put me in a different mood, taking me back to the days of cooking with my mother in my Thai kitchen. She liked to keep old utensils too, the only difference being that my mother didn't often use them, preferring to keep them in the cupboard for show. Once in a while, she would take them out to clean, her hands busily working while telling me the story of how and when each piece came into her possession.

My mother liked to clean the kitchen equipment at night. Sometimes when there is a live football match, she would watch the game and clean the kitchen antiques at the same time, to make good use of time.

Those old pieces have disappeared with the southern floods many years ago. Our old things and old photographs all vanished, much to my regret. Seeing Pasi's mother's old things brought tears to my eyes and I thought about my time with my family and our old things back in Thailand.

Another room which I loved was the workshop, which is a smaller construction separated from the main house. In it, there are many modern woodwork equipment. As a result, the big house had many beautiful wooden furniture pieces built by Pasi's father. Most Finn houses, even apartments, have a separate workshop because Finnish people like to create and mend pieces of furniture by themselves. Almost all schools taught woodwork to their kids, so most of them are skilled at woodwork and repair.

In Thailand, most of the repair work is the job of craftsmen who specialized in that vocation. Because labour in Thailand is so cheap, Thai men do not bother to learn about making or mending various things in the house. But the high cost of labour abroad is enough to motivate everyone to learn the basic skills and be self-reliant.

Another reason that I love to vacation at Pasi's parents' house is because I get to see the lifestyle of the Finns during summer and during the Christmas festival. It helps to make up for my loneliness from almost never getting to go back to visit my relatives in Thailand during the New Year or during Songkran.

Vacationing at their home reminds me of the small little things that make you happy in a family, and makes me miss Thailand a little less.

My confession

Another good point of vacationing at the beach house is that Pasi and I get to spend more time alone together. Pasi's parents and my eldest son usually volunteer to look after my younger son and baby daughter to allow Pasi and I to vacation together as a couple.

Pasi usually takes me on a drive to rent a bungalow by the beach, which is not far from the house, taking food and drinks with us. We like to go and sit by the beach to enjoy the breeze and talk about things that happened, whether it is about the kids or what we need to improve in our marriage. I really believe that talking openly with each other about everything is an essential part of marriage.

Since both of us come from different cultures and ways of thinking, talking with each other and trying to understand each other regularly has helped us to reduce our conflict and misunderstanding as a couple and most of all it stops us from repeating the same old mistakes.

It is also a good opportunity for Pasi and me to think about our sweet old memories. We usually talk about the love that we had for each other from the first day until now, and I usually take this time to let my husband know how much I love him and care about him. I tell him, *"I can take care of you. I would be your arms and your legs. I will take care of you until death do us part."* Pasi seems touched by this and it seems to have made him love me even more.

Once, on the beach, I sang John Denver's *"Annie's Song"* to Pasi. It was the song we sang together the first time we met in Singapore. I felt that the lyrics conveyed my feelings the best. There is a part which goes :

"Come let me love you, Let me give my life to you, Let me drown in your laughter, Let me die in your arms, Let me lay down beside you, Let me always be with you, Come let me love you , Come love me again."

I have loved this song since before I met Pasi and I used to sing this song back in Thailand to the couples who came to listen to me sing (at that time I was a folk song singer at a hotel in Songkhla). I never thought that I would have the chance to use this song for myself. The year after that, I used this song to accompany my speech when I gave a talk under the title, *"My Story."* I truly believe that love will get us both through many obstacles and I hope that other couples will get the chance to confess their love for each other as often as we used to do. Tomorrow might be too late.

Another Finn man that I love and the nickname "Golden Daughter-In-law"

If the Finn man that I love the most is my husband, there is another Finn man that has stolen my heart, and that man is no other than my husband's father!

I adore and worship Pasi's father as if he were my own father. In my opinion, he is the perfect man - kind, family oriented and loving to all his children and grandchildren. Even though I am not his real daughter, he treats me like I was his own daughter.

Whenever I am sick, he would take care of my medication. Whenever I cook, he comes to stand close by to help and to take out the garbage. Whatever help I needed, he would ask and he would always be on the lookout to see what the rest of the family needed. When he finds out that we are coming to visit, he would cook us a meal and wait in anticipation. As soon as we arrive he would come to take everyone's coats and prepare the meal. We only had to sit down and eat. At the same time he would constantly monitor the family and serve us food.

Whenever I look at him, I can't help but think of my own father back in Thailand. If my father was still around, he would be so proud to see me happy in a family that had somebody else taking care of me in his place. He would be so happy to see his youngest granddaughter. What a shame it was that he passed so soon. Whenever Pasi's father takes care of us so well, I can't help but think of my own father, and whenever I think about my father, I make a new promise to myself to take care of Pasi's father as well as I can to make up for the fact that I will never get to do that with my own father again.

I would often cut their fingernails and toenails, and give Pasi's mother and father a haircut when we visit the beach house, until both of them had to say, *"I've never been treated so well in my life"*. They nicknamed me *"Golden Daughter-in-law"*, which made me so pleased when I heard it. Even Pasi turned to me and whispered, *"I love you very much."*

Both of his parents usually express their gratitude that I am such a good daughter-in-law, but actually I have to thank them for bringing up such a good husband to me and making me one of the most enviable girls in Finland. I have to thank them too for being so kind to me and always being on my side.

My beloved father

Ever since I was young, until now and until the end of my life, I have always had my father, Pratuang Jitnarong, in my heart. I am closer to my father than my mother, since my mother was spending a lot of time working at our family business. My father worked for the Electricity Generating Authority of Thailand, and therefore had predictable hours in which he could take care of all the kids.

More than that, my father still found the time to help my mother cook as well. He was truly the head of the family who took care of everything: the finances, our education, our family business. He was the chauffer, driving my mother to work and sending us to school, and he was always a source of inspiration and help whenever we had school activities.

Out of all of the children, I was the one with the most problems. My school supplies had to be different from everybody else's. If the school had a rule for us to wear pleated skirts, I took an iron the skirts and ironed out all the pleats. The material that the skirts were made of had to be different from everyone else because I demanded chiffon with an inside lining, which was more costly and complicated to make of course.

I was stubborn beyond belief and my father had to relent and take me to the tailor's, with me talking over the design with the tailor and him forking out the cash. My two elder brother and sister never caused a problem or a headache and never made trouble for my parents. They were content to wear the normal uniforms which could be bought at a local store. My father's loving me and spoiling me might have caused my brother and sister some source of concern in thinking that he did not love us equally, but that was not the case at all. He loved us all equally, but his extra care and attention for me probably came from wanting to cut out my constant whining and troublemaking.

After we all graduated and found jobs, my father still worried about us constantly - our diet, our finances and our wellbeing. My elder brother and sister never had any problems, but I was the troublemaker once again. Whichever corner of the country I ended up in, my father would send me food and all sorts of supplies to make my life easier, even clothes for me to wear.

When I was singing in the Northern part of the country, my parents still ran a boutique in Hat Yai district, Songkhla province. My father's concern for me, worrying that I wouldn't have any nice clothes to wear, made him send many beautiful pieces of garments without my mum's knowledge. In his care package he sent instant noodles, canned goods, rice, soap, toothpaste, as if I was going off to war.

After seeing the goods he sent, my neighbours made fun of me and said I was an overgrown kid who never grew up, but when I opened the box, gratitude overwhelmed me. In the box, my father would write me a note. He said that I should be patient and diligent towards my music. He suggested that I found difficult songs to sing, and to sing in many languages to increase my chances of finding work and to become a leading singer. I always did what he suggested, and everything turned out exactly as he said. My singing career prospered and my salary was raised.

When I was pregnant with my first baby, he took me to prenatal care and was nearby when I gave birth. When I woke up, the first face that I saw was his face. He showed so much attention and care that the nurses thought that he was the baby's father.

When I opened my own restaurant, my father cheered me on and named the restaurant Busarakam, which meant wisdom, intelligence, bravery, wealth, and prosperity. From the meaning of the word I knew that he always meant well for me, and it always upsets me when I think of him being gone, without a final goodbye, but I know that he would have said "I will love you and care for you forever", and I want to tell him that I love and worship him more than anything in the world and I will never forget him.

The luckiest woman in the world

Who is the luckiest woman in the world? I used to think that I was the luckiest woman, but one woman has beaten me to the title. That woman is Pasi's mother.

Pasi's mother lived a very interesting life. She is a retired teacher and a talented artist. Her beautiful paintings adorn the walls of their home, and more than that, she is a wonderful singer. It seems like Pasi's mother and I shared many common interests. We both liked to draw and sing. She likes to read and is a talented cook. Therefore, she was very happy that I was her daughter-in-law.

If we dig down into why I liked to read and cook and create handicrafts, all these things come from my parents, who both loved to read and loved all kinds of arts, whether it is singing, decorating, design, Thai foods, desserts, etc. All of these things were passed onto me and Pasi's mother was very pleased to learn this when we first met each other.

Every time I went to stay with Pasi's parents, she would bring out old photographs and proudly show them to me. They were photos of when she was a child up until she was a young woman. She told me about the time she was 4 years old and had to go through the war. At that time, Finland was at war with Russia and the whole country was in hardship. Food was so scarce that there was a ration system. She did not have enough clothes to wear to school and no shoes. Some homes were surrounded by bomb craters. I was not surprised that she is in the habit of living modestly until today.

Pasi's mother is the luckiest woman to have Pasi's father as her soulmate. Ever since I moved to Finland, I saw that she was quite ill and started not being able to move around freely. Pasi's father took care of the house and his wife at the same time. However, he never expressed any displeasure and took care of his wife wholeheartedly.

I learned that Pasi's mother had been sick for 20 years. Lately, she had to use an oxygen tank to help her sleep during the night. She had pains at night-time and was wheelchair bound, but she remained strong and took care of her health diligently. She had great encouragement from Pasi's father, who was by her side the entire time, giving her amazing strength to fight her illness. Love really does have healing powers!

My first son

Of all the people who had an impact on my life, and people who made me learn, gave me wisdom and made me see life as it is, my eldest son **Kittipong Jitnarong** has to be amongst one of them.

Nokweed or Kittipong Jitnarong followed me to Finland at the age of 9. At that time I was so overjoyed that Pasi allowed me to bring my eldest son from my ex-husband to come and live with us.

Nokweed seemed excited to be living in a new country and Pasi's family welcomed him into the family. Everyone was prepared to help him with his studies and activities, which made me a lot less worried about his future.

When I was pregnant with my second child and had to go to the hospital for a C-section, he was excited to have a little brother and even cooked food to bring for me at the hospital because he was scared that I wouldn't like hospital food. The food that he cooked was very tasty too.

After that, I was so busy with raising my second child that I didn't have enough time to talk to Nokweed as I should have, but from what I noticed, he loved going to school and had no trouble settling in. I called on him a lot to help with the baby, and he did not show any signs on being bored when I asked him to do so. Actually, that was just the exterior and my own conclusions. I never asked my son how he felt and what he wanted. I only thought that he didn't seem to have any problems, which meant that he was doing fine.

Until the day that he graduated from middle school came… as parents, Pasi and I had to attend the school event. It was the first time that I got to attend his school event and I was very happy to find out that Nokweed had won some prize money for doing well in his exams.

During the student's performance, Nokweed, who was the lead singer, said *"I dedicate this song as a surprise for my mother"*, and then sang Diana Ross's *"Do You Know Where You're Going To?"* which is one of my favourite songs that I always sang around the house. When I heard my son's beautiful voice, it brought tears to my eyes because I never realized that my son was such a talented singer. Other parents came to congratulate me and express their admiration. They told me that I was lucky to have such a talented child and that I had brought him up well.

Their praise made me feel so ashamed because I didn't even know what song he was going to sing and why he could sing it so well. When we got home, I asked him where he learned to sing and since when. His answer shocked me and made me so sad. Nokweed told me that the school had sent home a parent's report to let the parents know what is going on, but because I didn't know Finnish, I made it Pasi's job to deal with it. Pasi was always too occupied with work so he didn't go to all the school events. When Nokweed didn't get a consistent response, he didn't show us any more reports, because he knew that no one would be able to go.

Since Pasi and I didn't participate in the school activities, we didn't know about his progress. I chastised myself for not having enough time for my son, thinking that finding him good food, good clothes and providing him with a good location is the best thing I could give him. I never listened to his problems, never hugged him to tell him I loved him, and never encouraged him. Even with school work, I never asked if he was having problems because I was too busy teaching the other children, who are younger than Nokweed.

I used to wonder why Nokweed never had any problems with homework. Every day I saw him sitting quietly doing homework without asking me or Pasi. His answer made me even sadder. He said *"If I ask you, you wouldn't know because it's in Finn. If I ask Pasi, I hardly speak to him during the day, so I don't dare to. I would rather ask the teacher at school."* Everything he said was true. Pasi spoke very little, so when he met a child who was not so talkative like Nokweed, both of them were hardly speaking to each other, as if they were living in different households.

The whole situation was my fault. I never asked how he felt and never noticed what problems he had. I made up my mind to correct my mistakes. I explained to Nokweed how much I love him and how he mean the world to me. I apologized to my son for not taking close care of him and promised him that I would take better care of him. I understood that I could only make him see what I meant when I started acting the way I said I would. Since that day, I was very careful not to hurt his feelings, and constantly tell him how much I love him and how no love would be greater that I have for him.

Now I realize that bringing up a child is such delicate work. Parents have to dedicate their heart and soul to shape the child's experience in every way, especially their mind. I was lucky to discover my mistake early and be able to fix them, but there are many other Thai women in my situation and have had to end up sending their children to foster homes.

Most of the children who follow their mothers abroad suffer from language barriers and adjusting to their new environment. If the mother doesn't try to understand the problem, it will only grow and grow. Therefore I want to suggest to mums who want to bring their children with them to prepare them for the changes they will experience, as well as asking themselves whether they understand their children well enough. If they run into problems, they have to fix it together and not push the child away into foster care, because that will only make their suffering even worse.

I want to encourage a lot of Thai mothers in Finland who are going through this problem. I hope you can find a good solution and I believe that a mother's love can bring everyone out of any major obstacles, as long as you don't give up.

What to do after you graduate

Many of my friends used to tell me that they were prepared to spend whatever amount of money was required as long as they could have a chance to attend the graduation ceremony of their children. A lot of the children had to do whatever their mums had designed for them without knowing what they liked to do and what their talents are. Some were too scared of angering their mothers and getting cut off from university fees so they studied those subjects hoping to bring home a degree for their mother.

I was one of the people who used to think that. I had hoped that my children would be able to go to university in Finland, which is not an easy thing even though my son was usually amongst the top of his class and never got less than 9 in his grades. I hoped that he would get a Ph.D. Actually I was the selfish one who wanted to see him get a doctorate to satisfy my own needs, even though I claimed to be doing it for his future. I never asked him whether he liked to study and wanted to follow the path that I had designed for him.

When he failed to get into university, I was displeased and thought that he did not pay attention to his studies and do not read up enough, but I didn't want to scold my son. Instead I asked him whether the exam was difficult. My son replied that preparing for university took no less than 1-2 years and a lot of studying. Once you enter university, you also have to study hard until you graduate. He said that his friends who are attending university told him that if he knew what he wanted to be, to follow that path to make the university studies more structured.

He wanted to pursue vocational studies more than attend university, since he had a love for computers. He wanted to learn about techniques that he never knew about. When I heard my child say those things, I started to agree with him and thought that vocational studies could be one of the subjects that could be adapted to fit life, without having to go to university.

I have seen my friends with grown-up children with university degrees from famous universities hanging up on the wall. They are not working, claiming that the salary is too low and they are content to live off their parents. The parents are happy to see the children living close by, with university degrees hanging on the walls to show comers and goers that their children attended a good university. I didn't understand what good those degrees will do. For me, my thinking changed since I heard my child explain his logic to me. I was proud that he was studying a subject he enjoyed and doing a job he loves.

My children's happiness doesn't come from doing what makes me happy, but comes from them fulfilling their own goals and getting a job they love. I think that every job in the world has to provide some source of joy to ensure that the job gets completed well. I saw my son going to school happy every day, and from that, indescribable happiness started to build and build inside my heart.

Skilled workmen

To me, skilled workmen are a very important part of society. I appreciate skilled craftsmanship, whatever it is. It sounds like you are an important person and you are needed in society. Skilled workmen in Finland are admired and earn a very good living. They can afford to eat lunch at restaurants every day and still go home to drink beers with their friends and family.

I see builders, road builders, plumbers and other blue collar uniforms that say a lot about the strength of the person wearing them and I think it is a suitable profession for men. Everyone gives them credit for their specialist skills and all of them have to go through rigorous training to be proficient in their field.

In Thailand, the picture is very different, showing you that Thailand still does not give too much importance to their vocational students and the skilled workmen of the future. Actually, in our daily lives, we cannot live without these people. However, much of the focus seems to be turned onto posh universities with expensive fees. That is why Thai society cannot progress and remains stagnant, staying in the same place.

If my home country had given some importance to these vocational mechanics, supporting new places of education to produce quality graduates, supported a new generation of professors to guide the students with techniques and know-how to let those who study in vocational schools know that being a mechanic should be a source of pride just as much as being in famous universities, I believe we wouldn't hear about students from vocational schools getting into fights with each other because they would take pride in themselves. In actual fact, Thailand can produce skilled workers who can design, tailor and invent things just as well as foreigners.

Nowadays there are so little skilled dressmakers. Those who have the right skills have a year-long waiting list. Despite the trendy design, by the time the work is completed it might be out of fashion. That is because no one wants to study in this field. 80% of university students want to study journalism, communication arts, or dream of having jobs as airhostesses or PR people for famous hotels. This kind of dream makes tailoring and dressmaking the least preferred choice that is only picked after all other options have been exhausted. Only then will the youth choose to study tailoring, beauty school or technical school. When there is no passion for the subject, the result is that the skills naturally suffer as well.

I wish to see Thailand with a multitude of leading skilled workers who have creative ideas - whether it is the brilliant chefs who can not only cook food, but also know how to carve it, as well as know the nutritional content, the history of the fruit and vegetables that they use, become dietitians that can consult customers about their health and diet, as well as know the basic dishes of food all from all over the world. All of these things are essential to the career of preparing food.

Skilled workers in Thailand are an ignored profession even though Thai people are just as capable as any around the world. It is a shame to let popularity and consumerism make us overlook these professions. Most of these jobs are frowned upon as not cool, and are the least preferred choices by youngsters.

I wonder how we would live without all of these skilled people. Whenever I go back to Thailand, I always pay a visit to my father's friend, who is a tailor, to get many shirts made for Pasi. Every time, he would complain about the lack of skilled help even though he has so much work at hand from institutes, universities, nurses and hotels, who hire him to make their uniform, making a large amount of money. He has to tell them that he can't finish the work in time and he can't accept any more because he has no help. I asked him why he cannot find help and he reply was that no one from the young generation wants to be a tailor. Everyone wants to go to university and find other jobs. What about his children? I asked. He replied that he had sent them abroad to study, so I kept quiet and thought to myself that if his children didn't want to study vocational subjects or they didn't like what their parents did, they had other alternatives such as teaching or consulting for universities using their skills and passing on the knowledge to younger generations. I told him my ideas and the answer was that he had no time and didn't want to start because he was afraid of not being able to do it.

I felt sorry for the loss of knowledge from my father's friend. One day he is no longer with us, and the techniques and craftsmanship will die with him. For me personally, encouraging a person to grow according to their potential is the most important thing of all. It does not matter if that potential ends with a university degree, a technical college degree, or a vocational degree. The most important thing is for the parents to have an open mind and not be rooted to the old ways in order to encourage the younger generation to follow their dreams. The parents' support is the most important lifeline that will help youngsters to pave their own way and find their own path away from society and from the trappings of their minds.

A lesson for the ladies

When I first got married, I thought to myself that it was love when actually I didn't even know the meaning of love very well. I only thought that when two people like each other and look suitable for spending their lives together, that should result in marriage so that their parents can be proud. After spending married life together, nothing turned out the way I expected. That would be the best way to explain my first marriage. At that time, I was focused on making money so I didn't pay as much attention to the family as a good housewife should do. I thought that you should find as much money as possible, and when you have a lot of money, you will have time to think about yourself and your own happiness later.

I hardly ever did my wifely duties. I pushed aside the duties of taking care of my family to the workers or the chef at my restaurant, even though I was a fantastic cook. Very seldom did I cook for my family because I thought that my time was precious and I shouldn't be wasting time doing these little things.

That was my biggest mistake in my first marriage. My first husband and I hardly ever got to sit down and have a meal together because I always put the priority on the customers. If a customer walked in, I was ready to abandon my dinner companion without thinking that it was a really selfish thing to do and it was driving a wedge into our relationship.

One day I found that my ex-husband was with my best friend. She had more time for him. At that time I blamed other people and thought that I was betrayed, without thinking what I had done anything wrong. Now looking back, I find that I couldn't blame anyone but myself because at that time I overlooked the most important thing, which was my family.

I understood this deeply when I read a book by a monk in a Thai temple in Perth, Australia. He told the story of *"The Mexican Fisherman"* for us to think about what is really important in life.

In the story, in a quiet fishing village in Mexico, an American tourist came to vacation and observed a fisherman unloading his catch of the day. The American was a highly successful professor of business administration at a famous American university.

He couldn't help but offer a little piece of advice to the Mexican fisherman without asking for any consulting fee.

"Hey," The American began, "Why did you stop fishing so early in the morning?"

"I have caught enough fish for the day, signor," the Mexican replied good-naturedly.

"I have enough to feed my family, and I have a little bit left over to sell. I'm going to have lunch with my wife and take a little nap. In the afternoon I'll get up, play with my kids, and after dinner I'm going to the bar to have a little tequila and play guitar with my friends. That is enough for me, signor."

"My dear friend, listen to me." The business professor started to say.

"If you stay out in the ocean until noon, you will easily catch twice more fish. You can sell the leftovers, save up for six to nine months and buy a bigger and better boat, and you can also hire more crew. Then, you could catch four times as much fish. Think about how much money you will make!"

"In a year or two, you will have money to invest in a second boat, and you can hire another team of fishermen. If you follow this business plan, in six or seven years, you will own an entire fleet of fishing boats which will be very impressive indeed"

"Just imagine that. You can move your office to Mexico City or even L.A. In just three or four in L.A., you can enter the stock market, make yourself CEO, take a high salary with large benefits, or you can opt for a large amount of shares instead."

"Then in just a few years, listen carefully here, you can start a plan to buy all your shares back, which will make you a billionaire, I can assure you. I'm a professor at a very famous business school in the United States. I know about these things."

The Mexican fisherman listened carefully to everything the American said. When the man finished, he asked, "Signor Professor, what would I do with all those millions of dollars?"

That was baffling for the American professor because he never thought about such a long-sighted angle to his business plan.

Off the top of his head he thought about what someone might do with such a lot of money. "Friend, when you have that much money, you no longer have to work. Yes, that's it. You won't have to work for the rest of your life. You can buy a little villa in a picturesque village, like this one, and buy a small boat to go fishing in the morning. You can come and have lunch with your wife every day and have a little nap with nothing to worry about."

"In the afternoon you can spend quality time with your little ones, and then go out in the evenings to play the guitar and have a little tequila with your friends. With that much money, you can stop working and live a relaxing life."

"But Signor Professor, what is what I do every day already."

Why oh why do we believe that we must work hard to get rich before finding the pleasure in life?

When I read the whole story, I finally understood that if I had found the time for my family without thinking about getting rich and waiting to have everything to be happy, I wouldn't have lost my family. Now, I have incorporated all of the teachings I had learned into my daily life. I decided to sell my restaurant and work less in order to find time to spend with my family, to take care of the kids and my husband, and most of all, to take care of myself.

Twenty years ago, I worked hard without caring for my health. It's time to watch my children and grandchildren grow up and find a perfect family life. More than that, it is time to make my dream come true, that is, writing this book and going back to Thailand to take care of my mother, who is waiting for me with every breath. If I waited for the chance to get rich before going back to take care of her, I might lose that chance forever if my mother cannot wait for me.

106 The Foreign In-Law ส.ไก่ต่างแดน

Chapter 6
The star of Finland

New social scene

In the past years, I had the chance to participate in many local activities, which introduced me to new friends and a new social scene in Finland. There are many non-governmental organizations that are open to foreigners to participate, for example the Finland Red Cross, Women's groups and many religious groups.

Volunteering is the most highly praised profession in Finland because those who do have to give up their time without expecting anything in return. As well as this, they have to be enthusiastic and have to be able to work with others. Apart from all the non-governmental organizations of Finland, even Thai people have their own associations and volunteer groups to hold interesting activities during annual festivals, for example holding Thai classes, Thai cooking classes, street fairs and Thai cultural performances.

Having the opportunity to spread Thai culture, whether it is expressed through on-stage performances, fruit carving, artificial flowers or other handicrafts is a source of pride for my family back in Thailand and for my family in Finland. The most important thing is to be able to do activities with other people who are not from the same country. I could not hold back the feeling that I wanted to tell other people in the world about my culture, and they shared their culture with me. All of them were beautiful and interesting and added to my knowledge. This knowledge would stay with the Finnish people, who are lucky enough to be in touch with all of the cultures of all the different countries.

I thought this was a good thing and helps to create harmony with all the different races and groups. I had more friends and got many great opportunities from all the different organizations.

My second home, Caisa Cultural Center

Another place that had the most importance to my life in Finland and became my second home is the Caisa Cultural Centre. It was a place to meet and exchange ideas with the foreigners who were living in Finland. It was a refuge for foreigners and helped many underprivileged people find jobs and make progress in their lives.

I found a great job partly through the recommendation of the cultural producers of the centre, many of whom were my very good friends. I was particularly good friends with Oge and Kitari, who are kind and generous people and always willing to help all foreigners. When they found that I was good at singing Thai songs, they gave me the chance to really shine on stage. I felt like Caisa was my second home and is the place where many hearts come together in Finland.

Apart from the charming producers at Caisa, I also had two dear friends who are in charge of the light and sound on the performance stage, who are Jimmy and Gary. Every time I was on stage, I was confident that I would sound good and look great because of my two talented friends helping me backstage, and they never let me down. I was always impressive onstage.

On the big stage in Finland

The sound of His Majesty's composition *"Sang Tian"* echoed through the Caisa Cultural Center, Finland, Helsinki. It was the arrangement by Khun Sarawut Supanyo, the famous Thai artist who graciously produced 13 songs, all of which show off the Thai king's immense talent.

Having the chance to perform Thai music in front of foreigners was like a dream. They sat in still silence listening to Thai music without knowing the meaning of the words, but everyone was polite and tried to listen using the basis of art and music, where language can never be a barrier. The knowledge that I had within myself is being used to its full potential. My singing job in Thailand made me a singer in Finland, how unbelievable!

Many Thai singers who live abroad do not have the chance or the courage to do what I did. When the Kassandra choir offered the opportunity for foreigners to show off what they do onstage, I offered my services, confident that a Thai song can make foreigners know and absorb Thai culture with Thai language. Why did I think that?

In Thailand, in the past and presently, there are many influences from foreign songs, whether Chinese, Indian, Malaysian, British, Korean, Lao and many more. Thai people can sing them and like to listen to them until they become a popular hit even though they only understand 20-30% of the song. Other than that, they listen to the melody and beat, which can entertain Thai people quite a lot.

By contrast, in Finland, there isn't that much foreign music playing even though there is quite a foreign population here. As a Thai, I would have been pleased if there was a radio station or TV program presenting Thai music. I used to talk to many of my foreign friends about this and they also had the same opinion.

Finland extends its kindness to the world by accepting refugees of war from the world over. These people each have their own culture and probably want to listen to their own music. At the same time, Finns have the opportunity to absorb different cultures and enjoy the different music of the world.

By offering myself as part of the choir or even getting on stage to sing Thai songs, I wanted to disseminate Thai culture and Thai music to my other friends in the world. Many Finnish people liked Thai music and said that they enjoy the melody and the beautiful music even though they did not understand the language. The body language that I expressed allowed them to understand the music quite easily.

For each performance, my Thai costume is without a doubt the first thing that I prepare - even my hair and my makeup had to go with my dress. When it came to looking my best, I never disappointed. I pulled out all the stops without caring how much I was getting paid, just as long as I looked like Miss Thailand when I was onstage. That was enough for a singer like me. As for dramatic expressiveness, 10 years' experience is enough to guarantee that I would not be a letdown for my country.

As I expected, the Thai music was mentioned and appreciated by the crowd. They came to congratulate me and ask for my autograph. After being a singer for 10 years, no one had ever asked for my autograph since I wasn't a famous star, but in Finland, I received the highest honour from the audience without expecting it. It was like an unexpected dream, especially with Pasi standing by, good naturedly watching his wife signing autographs.

I think that foreigners and Finns alike want to absorb different cultures, but it is a pity that organizations which support foreigners are not fully supported. Every time foreigners come forward to display their own culture, they get very little compensation so they cannot do as much as they would like. In my experience, there are many talented foreigners living in Finland waiting to show off their beautiful culture, if only they got the right chance.

Joining a choir with foreigners

For a while, I joined a choir for foreigners, which was a valuable experience. Part of it was letting others know about Thai culture. Most of my friends had only heard about the bad side of Thailand and Thai women. When they got to know me, they got to know another part of Thailand and their attitude towards Thai people changed. I took this opportunity to tell them about my home and was a great promoter for all the great places to visit Thailand.

When it came to choosing songs for the choir, I chose the composition *"Chata Cheewit", "Pan Din Kong Rao", "Duang Jai Gub Kwam Rak" and Chao Phraya* by The Impossible as the pieces for the choir. My foreign friends were astounded by His Majesty the King's ability for composition.

To get my new friends to really feel and get into Thai culture, I embarked on a mission to cook Thai food for all of them to taste. Most were impressed by the taste and the giving culture of Thai people. At that time, I felt like I had got through a little opening in the wall that blocked different cultures from each other, and I felt that I could touch their hearts.

I maybe I could not change all of their negative prejudices, but they were certainly more open to Thailand. So I felt that joining the choir was very beneficial because I got to use my Thai charm to impress the foreigners and made a lot of new friends.

Singing Nawamin Maha Racha on television

Another performance that I was very proud of is singing Nawamin Maha Racha on Finnish national television. At the same time, I gave an interview about Thailand and Thai women on air as well.

I believed that I helped to build a good reputation for Thai women who have married Finns and moved to Finland. Pasi's family in particular seem very pleased with this Thai in-law. I felt happy to do good for Thai society and help to enhance the image of Thai women in foreigner's eyes.

Our Vision Contest

When the *"Our Vision"* Contest was organized for the first time in Finland, the organisers at Caisa pleaded with me to join because there were many countries participating. I agreed to participate without any expectations of any prizes in this contest, since the song I was using was in Thai, whereas most other contestants selected English songs.

I chose a Thai song because I wanted Thai music to be known to everyone else. Even if I chose an English language song, my accent could hardly compete with a European or other countries that use English as their second language.

I decided to enter to create inspiration for other Thai generations who have also moved abroad. I wanted to encourage them to be expressive and show off their talents so that other foreigners could witness it.

I intended to sing *"Siam Muang Yim"* from Thailand's most famous country singer, Poompuang Duangchan. Even though I only had 2 weeks to prepare, I was not worried because I knew that my chances of winning was next to nothing.

My goal for this performance was to bring Thai music to the international stage and get other foreigners to experience the beauty of Thai music. I would already consider that a big victory for a little Thai woman like me.

Not winning but being selected

I didn't win, but I was selected... I was contacted by Kitari, one of the cultural producers of Caisa, to help promote the Euro Vision Song Contest Helsinki 2007, which was being hosted by Finland.

This activity was held in front of a large shopping mall called Kamppi. An African singer and I were selected to sing to promote the Eurovision contest.

I was honoured and a little surprised at the same time, since there were many other foreigners who won the competition and who were more talented than me. My other singer friends were all saying that I was the most suitable person for the job since no one has ever been disappointed when they see me on stage - my Thai costumes are always the most beautiful and my songs unique, not sounding like any other they've heard before. They agreed that I was best suited for promoting this event. When I looked down at my Thai costume, I couldn't help but think that maybe the Thai costume is really part of the reason I was chosen, just like my friends said. My Thai costumes were always beautiful and varied. I wouldn't be wrong if I said my Thai costume saved the day.

Although I don't really know the real reason the panel chose me, I was happy to get the chance to spread Thai culture by dressing up in my Thai costume and singing to foreigners. Thank you to Kitari, the cultural producer of Caisa, for seeing the value of Thai music and Thai customs.

Culture

As I said in the beginning, I am a keen learner, or, it could be said that I am quite the busybody. Whatever anybody else did, I liked to watch and learn or try to remember how they did it. However, not everything can be learned just by observation or just from watching YouTube.

My need to absorb Thai culture and appreciate the value of Thai culture as a Thai person required me to make a serious effort to learn many skills, including singing, which many people think is just a natural talent that requires a bit of practice, and that anyone can be a singer.

I used to think that too, but when I saw other friends in the same profession who were better at what they did, I started to ask myself, *"What can I do to sing as well as they can?"*

I started taking singing lessons with a qualified teacher and discovered that there are many things I did not know, such as breathing techniques or learning to phase things in the right way. That was the beginning of my efforts to learn things correctly by myself. I wanted to learn Thai dance as well as singing, so I went to study Thai dance with one of the most famous teachers from the southern provinces. Because I come from the southern region of Thailand, I was most interested and very proud to carry forward the traditions of my home province: the Norah Thai dance.

Studying intensively and training with a teacher made me realize that Thai dance was not as easy as it looks. On the first day, every part of my body ached so badly that I nearly gave up, but my curiosity got the better of me. I finally got through the classes and I try to practice it constantly. I had the chance to bring the southern culture and tradition to Finland, which made me very happy and very proud. While I was performing, I could hardly believe that all of the audience were foreigners. There were some Thai people in the crowd, but not many.

Likewise, when I go to demonstrate fruit and vegetable carving at various places in Finland, even at events that are attended by national leaders, I am the only Thai woman standing up and putting on a carving show, dressed in my national costume. For me, it is a dream come true. Passers-by can never resist taking a look and asking me for a photograph.

While I am carving the pieces, there are many questions about the method and a lot of admiration for the pieces that I lay out on display. The audience cannot tell that I haven't slept all night because I had to carve many pieces of fresh fruits and vegetables overnight to use as decoration for the show. It was very important that they remain fresh.

Every exhibition was time-consuming and required delicate precision to execute it perfectly. I also combined the art of flower arrangement to make one harmonious and beautiful display.

Being given this task is very important to me, whether it was shown at weddings, birthdays, celebrations, company launches or even funerals, doing these things to add the final touches allows foreigners to truly appreciate the value of Thai art and culture.

No matter where you are in the world, if you see the sign for fruit and vegetable carving, you can be sure that there is a Thai person around there. That is why I do not hesitate to bring this symbolic Thai art to the world every chance I get. Every time I do, the compensation hardly makes up for the costs, but for me, doing what I love and what I have tirelessly studied for is a source of pride and joy. Even people who are close to me, like Pasi and his family, or my family, friends and teachers at home, also take equal pride in my work. I believe that there are many Thai people living abroad who are talented and if they also show off Thai culture to other foreigners, they would also feel the same way I do. Being a foreign in-law for me does not mean coming here to have a new family or alternative choices: it means that I get to use my Thai culture and my Thai ways to show the world that we are a civilized nation.

The Thai sense of pride in our country, religion and our King cannot be removed from our blood. Wherever we are in the world, the millions of Thai people living abroad cannot let the chance go by without telling the world that we are Thai and we are proud to be Thai.

The Thai Women's Exhibition was appointed and supported by the Africans and African-Europeans Association to hold an exhibition on Thailand on 5th March 2013. At that time, I did not have much time to prepare, since Thailand was selected to perform first, followed by Indonesia, the Philippines and Africa. Therefore, the sourcing of all the equipment was done in a rush. Fortunately, I received a lot of help from Thai restaurateurs, who were my friends and surrogate family. They kindly allowed me to take whatever I wanted to for the decorations. Some of them even drove the decorations over to me themselves.

Most of all, the Thai restaurants in Finland supported us by delivering boxed Thai food to the foreign student volunteers, who were our staff at the exhibition. They provided the exhibition's information to the attendees from day one until the last day.

Wherever we are, Thai people show generosity and compassion to each other and support everything which benefits our country. I thank you all from the bottom of my heart.

While I was monitoring the event and putting on the carving show, there were many people who were interested in Thailand's exhibition. The exhibition included Thai kitchen equipment and seasonings, Thai books, Thai language, traditional Thai costumes, the Norah dance performance, carving equipment, a soap carving exhibition, and many more handcraft shows, such as turning unused household items into gifts, bags, earrings, belts, necklaces, cups, photo frames decorated with fish scales and hosiery, and many more. It showed foreigners that Thai people are talented and whatever we are, we can use the knowledge we have to add benefit, as well as help to promote Thai culture and tradition. Even though there was not much time to preplan for this event, receiving help from my fellow Thai citizens made me realize that Thai people living abroad want to support and promote Thai culture as much as possible. Those who could not personally help out sent equipment and food to support us. This also shows another Thai culture - generosity and helping each other, wherever we are. The exhibition was a very valuable lesson for me. For example, working with foreigners for one full month created friendships that have lasted until today, and in the future I hope that I will get another opportunity to bring Thai culture to into the spotlight once again.

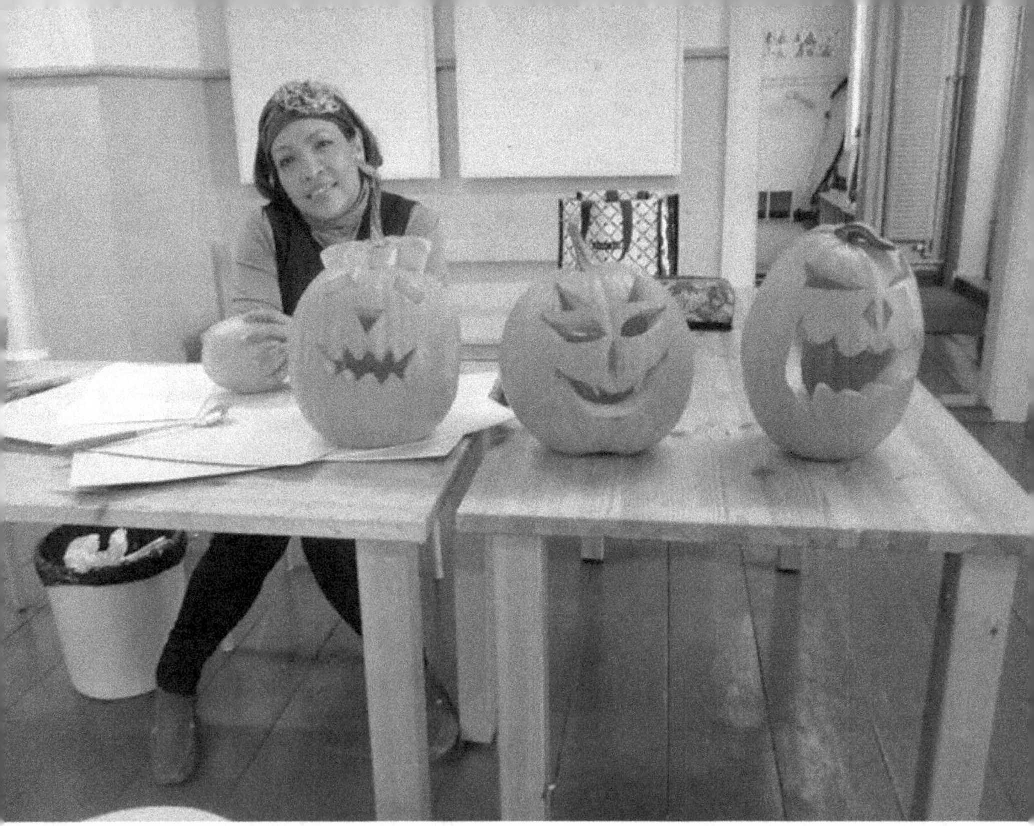

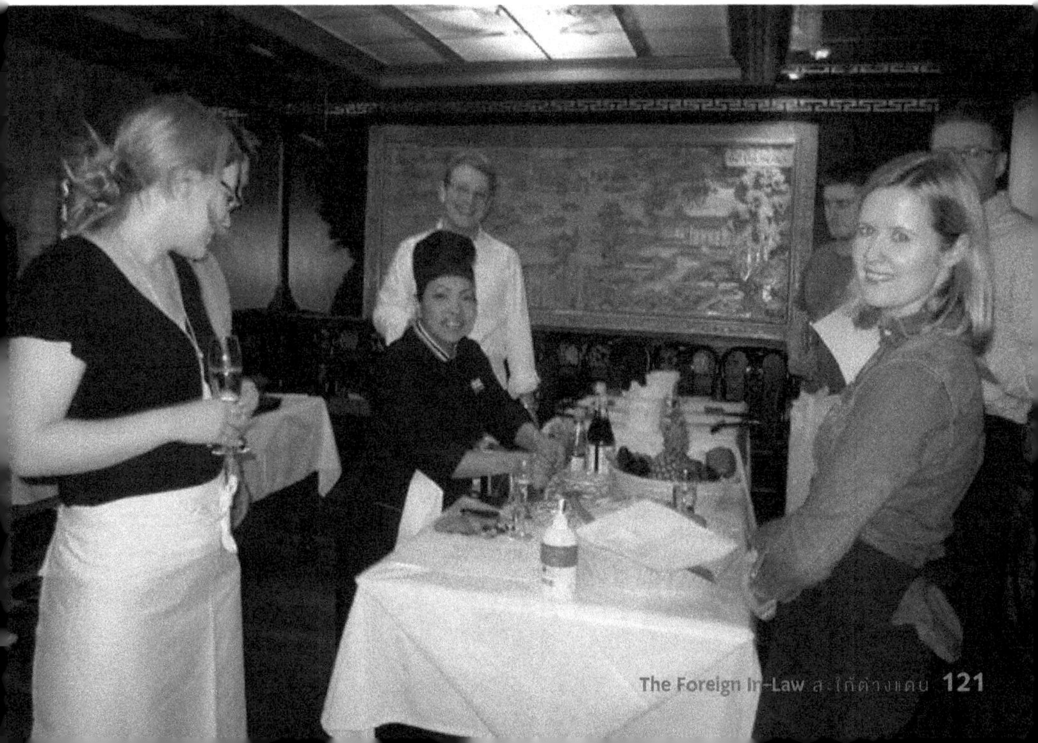

Chapter 7
Giving back to my motherland

Chairwoman for the Finnish Thai Association

I never thought that I would get such a high honour, that is, becoming the chairwoman for the Finnish Thai Association. The role of this position was to promote Thai culture abroad, as well as hold activities with other organizations and the embassy to carry out this goal. As well as this, the Chairwoman had to do things that would benefit Thai people and Thai society as much as possible. I was overjoyed to get this position, because this would be my chance to do some good for my country while I was abroad, even though I felt a little worried about finding time for my family.

At that time, my third baby was still small and needed close care and attention. I asked Pasi for advice and luckily he understood that I wanted to work for my country, so he gave up his time of relaxation after work to help me take care of the kids so that I could focus on working for the association. I was very touched by his sympathy and understanding.

The chairwoman's work was a heavy task because you have to work with government offices and other organizations. As well as this, all of the activities had to be supported by the Thai Embassy in Sweden, especially in the days when Finland did not have a Thai embassy.

After the Thai Embassy in Finland was established, it made work much easier because the ambassador and other government offers were available to lend a helping hand. The association's work has progressed much further than before, which is very good news for Thai people living abroad in Finland.

A night honouring His Majesty in Helsinki

I had the opportunity to hold the first event honouring His Majesty the King. It was called *"The night of the musical compositions of His Majesty King Bhumibol Adulyadej of Thailand."* Inspired by working with the international choir, I asked the talented singers to individually sing a solo, and the songs they would sing were His Majesty the King's compositions.

The international singers had to take 3-4 full months to practice singing the Thai songs, with me as their close supervisor. Every care had to be taken not to mess up the words or lyrics from the original composition, which turned out to be a very tough job, but everyone was determined and committed to this performance. The result was a night which impressed and excited the guests as well as Thai people in Finland, as well as the Thai embassy in Sweden.

The opportunity to do good for your country can be done in many ways, depending on your skills, your proficiency, and your readiness to do so. Most importantly, it depended on the support of the Thai community and the funding available. I believe that there are many Thai people who think like me, but due to their duties and roles, they cannot do everything their heart desires. For me, I got the chance to follow my desires when the opportunity presented itself, so I was very lucky indeed.

The benefactors

The Thai embassy in Sweden was a main supporting force in this event. I received a sum of money from the Ambassador of Thailand to Sweden, who at that time was His Excellency Apichat Chinwanno and Minister Counselor Siriporn Panupong. They were instrumental in giving advice and giving me encouragement until the event could be completed.

The costs in holding this night was very high because some of the things had to be ordered from Thailand, for example a portrait of His Majesty the King, which was 3x3 meters, as well as the decorations and costumes. As well as this there were other expenses in promoting the event, such as leaflets, posters and the printing of tickets, as well as a fee for arranging the music into a choral arrangement.

Luckily, my kind brother, Khun Pachai Jitnarong, was my coordinator in Thailand, just like every time. Pasi also took care of the other expenses that I had to pay for in advance. I can safely say that without the help of my brother and the financial help from my husband, that magical night could not have happened.

Another important person who I cannot forget to mention is my eldest son, who helped me to complete all the paperwork and follow up on all the other proceedings, as well as Pasi's friends, who videotaped the whole event. I have to thank all of my benefactors from the bottom of my heart.

The Thai and foreign artists

The night honouring His Majesty the King was held for the first time, the first of its kind in Finland, with numerous Thai and foreign artists attending, such as:

Khun Banyen Rakgaen, the queen of Mor Lam, a type of Thai country music from Thailand. She wowed the audience with her music and her beautiful Thai dancing.

Khun Chanida Kosai, who sang His Majesty's compositions so beautifully. It was refreshing to see the talent of Thai children living overseas.

Khun Anusri Issara, a Thai language and Thai dance teacher in Finland. She brought a Pong Lang, which entertained the audience so much. The liveliness of her performance was mentioned in relation to this event repeatedly. As well as that, it was hard to forget her unique smile.

Nam, a young talent, performed the Chui Chai Phram Thai dance so mesmerizingly in front of the international audience. As well as that, the Thai junior ballroom champion of Finland performed beautiful ballroom dances accompanied by the King's compositions.

As well as that, the Minister Counselor, Siriporn Panupong, sang the royal composition, *"Saeng Duen"*, in which she flew from Sweden just to rehearse for this occasion.

There were so many other Thai artists in attendance and I apologize for not being able to name all of them here because the list would simply be too long.

All of the other international artists who were participating in this event came from 15 different countries, and all of them appeared in their national costumes.

Our international choir performed *"Pan Din Kong Rao"* and *"Duang Jai Gub Kwam Rak"* in Thai. As well as this, the singers all performed their own solo of his Majesty's compositions in English. The Thai audience was left feeling very impressed.

The Ndioba group jazz band also did us the honour of performing His Majesty's composition. Bina Nkwazi, a famous Zambian singer, also perfomed *"Candle Lights Blue."*

Fatima Usman, from Nigeria and her daughter Winnie sang *"Love at Sundown"* together.

Peali Mitra, from India sang a song called *"Love in Spring."*

Ernie Raduch and Vilmi Lesmana from Indonesia performed *"Falling Rain"* and *"Blue Day."*

Veera Voima, from Finland, the director of our choral group and an accomplished singing instructor, performed *"No Moon."*

Hannah Wilson, from the United Kingdom, joined in with *"Near Dawn."*

And **Maija Marttiini** sang the composition entitled *"Magic Beams."*

The most important thing for this event was the hosts, where we had three hosts speaking three different languages. They were lively and filled the evening with laughter. That is, Ariya, the American host of Our Vision song contest. There was also a Thai host, a beautiful ex-air hostess, as well as a Finnish host who Kassandra sent to liven up the evening. All of these artists came to work for the event without expecting anything in return, leaving me speechless. Even now when we have the opportunity to meet, they still ask me *"When are you going to have another event to honour your King again? I want to go and sing for you, I really liked it, especially the royal compositions."* Hearing this makes me so proud, and I hope that I can organize a big event to bring such joy to everyone again in the future.

The attendees

It would be a shame not to mention those who attended the event as all the attendees honoured the event and were dressed up beautifully. Most of the gentlemen wore suits, and the ladies wore Thai costumes. The international guests were in evening gowns. The concert was held at Sibelius Akatemia Pohjoinen Rautatienkatu 9, Helsinki, which was a place for musical exhibitions and very suitable for this event.

After the concert, many people came to congratulate me and told me *"I wish you could hold this event again. Next time I'll bring my family"*, to which I replied *"If I did another one, I would make it much bigger and without ticket sales."* I want to hold an event where people can eat for free and watch free live performances. I know for sure that The Foreign In-Law part 2 will not have any ticket sales, have free food, and free entertainment. Please wait a while and there may be some good news!

Loss is Profit

In holding that event night, I made a loss as I did not have a contingency plan or Plan B. In everything, even when you are the best prepared, unprecedented mistakes can still occur.

That is, there were many attendees in the show, but half of them were guests from all walks of life. I gave particular importance to the performers, who volunteered to give up their efforts without taking payment. The only thing that I could reward them with was free tickets for their friends and family, as well as food. Nevertheless, I think that I was right to save the relationship rather than save money. If I should hold the event again or not, I still have lasting friendships and they would be ready to step in whenever required.

I took all of these things as lessons which would teach me to understand more about event organizing abroad, which is quite different from how it is in Thailand. Thus, I thought that this loss was my profit.

However, the thing that made me the most uncomfortable is that Pasi had to invest a lot of money. After the concert, Pasi hardly said a word to me. I think he was disappointed and upset that he believed me.

At that time, I felt like I was heartbroken. I was disappointed that I had let Pasi down, and I couldn't stop thinking about how I would get Pasi to understand that I didn't mean for things to end up this way. I was scared that Pasi would break up with me or ask for a divorce because I didn't know what he was thinking then. He was silent and didn't say much, so I was very anxious and worried.

After three days, Pasi started talking to me, probably because he couldn't stand to see my sad and woebegone face. He asked me to come back to being a wife and mother to our children. What had happened was not a grave unforgiveable mistake - I didn't go gambling or spend the money on something bad. On the contrary, I had worked hard and dedicated myself to my country, something which Pasi felt constantly, and the concert itself was a great success. Pasi told me that he never thought a small Thai woman like me could take on such a big job, which is not easy in a country that is unfamiliar to you. He was very proud of me, and that is a part of the reason that he came around.

Most importantly, Pasi told me that he loves me ne so much that he couldn't stand to see me plummeting deeper down into my sadness. Of course, every penny that he gave me was from his savings and anyone would feel bad for losing it, but Pasi said he would rather lose that money than lose his wife. When I heard him say that, tears came to my eyes. Pasi was so generous to me. This is another case where I felt that my loss was my profit. I lost money, but what I got back was the knowledge that my husband loves and cares for me and I got back to my warm loving family. That was more valuable than anything.

Doing good

While I was the chairwoman of the Finnish Thai Association, I was determined to do as much good for the Thai community in Finland as possible.

I learned that Thai people in Turku wanted to have a Thai temple there, since Finland had only one Thai temple in Helsinki and travelling from Turku to the temple took a long time. It would take 2 hours travelling by train. I consulted Khun Warisara or P' Daeng, who was familiar with Thai people in Turku to seek help from the Thai temple in Sweden to write to **Somdej Prayanwarodom of Wat Thepsirintarawas** about this matter.

I had the chance to travel to Thailand with P' Daeng to pay a visit to the highly revered monk, where I informed him of the needs of the Thai people in Turku. He was extremely merciful and sent a Thai monk to Turku to carry out Buddhist affairs. This was a great source of joy for the Thai people in Turku and nearby areas.

I was proud to have helped the Thai people in Finland as well as help to spread Buddhism in a foreign country. Currently, this Thai temple has been well looked-after by the Thai people in Turku and there are regular religious celebrations.

The key of a temple is to help Thai people abroad have spiritual guidance as well as to give Thai people the chance to make merit and meet with each other to exchange knowledge and opinions. For example, someone who has been living in Finland for a long time would have advice for those who have just arrived. Another benefit to Thai people is that the temple is a centre of learning, whether vocational or learning Thai language for a lot of Thai children who have been born abroad. After learning Thai culture and Thai history, they will also know that there is another country to which they belong.

One of the things I'd like to see is to have more Thai temples in Finland, since Thai people are so dispersed in so many different places. Sometimes these people need a place to call a home away from home, and one of the best things is the Thai temple, which can be a source of solace and merit-making as well as other activities. However, building a new temple is not an easy thing since the costs and responsibilities are endless. The person in charge must be giving, honest and dedicated to the religion in order to get through these hurdles.

One of the key elements of a Thai temple abroad is the monk. Monks who live abroad will have to study and be trained in the language, as well as the political, social, and historical context of that country, not only to spread this knowledge to the Thai community, but to communicate with other people who are interested in Buddhism as well. This knowledge can be spread across to other Thai generations loving abroad, getting the right knowledge and the right context with the right advice.

At the moment, Thailand's Chulalongkorn University has a politics, political science and foreign languages course for Buddhism, as well as a religious ambassador who travels aboard to spread religion, political history, as well as politics that people are struggling with all over the world. The monks can provide knowledge and a guiding light.

I watch Asia Update and many other Thai stations and I am overjoyed when I see monks speaking up about politics and providing a way out for Thai people, pointing out the difference between fairness and unfairness, as well as standing up for democracy without fearing for the powers that be anymore.

Right now, politics in Thailand and abroad needs monks to provide a light for the people to provide a counter balance that can help to save the country and to help Thai people become aware without giving up their own rights, and without failing to realize how important their voice is for the country. I really hope that Thai temples abroad can be a guiding light that shines on all Thai people and provide a tremendous force for change for the good of Thai people in the future.

An audience with the Crown Princess of Thailand

One night, the phone rang at 4 a.m. I was terrified, thinking that something bad had happened to my family in Thailand, but when I picked up the phone, I found that it was a call from the office of Her Majesty the Crown Princess' principal private secretary, notifying me of the schedule for an audience with the crown princess of Thailand!

I was selected for this high honour because of my work in honouring His Majesty the King in Helsinki, choosing his royal compositions and highlighting his royal duties, telling everybody about the benefits that His Majesty has bestowed upon the people of Thailand.

The office of Her Majesty the Crown Princess wished me to attend an audience with her Majesty to present the DVD of the event and to present a signing book by Thai Finnish people, with Her Excellency with Siriporn Panupong as the main person presenting my work to Her Majesty.

I was overwhelmed and was determined to donate a sum of money towards her Royal Projects, gathering my own savings and the contributions from other Thais living in Finland, as well as other donations from P' Daeng from Turku. I brought P' Daeng, my mother, my brother and my sister-in-law to accompany me on this occasion.

On 17 April 2006, at 8 a.m. at Dusidalai Hall, my party and I dressed in our finest clothes, to attend an audience with Her Majesty. I wore a Thai costume in a dark leafy hue, and my mother and sister-in-law both dressed up beautifully. When it was time for us to present our achievements and what we did, I had no need for any notes because I had memorized every single word off by heart.

When Her Majesty made her way towards me, my heart nearly stopped beating and my brain stopped functioning. I felt like was in a dream but Her Majesty's smiling face brought me to my senses and I started to give her a report of what I had done. She asked me whether Finnish was a hard language to learn, because Her Majesty wished to send some Thai students to Finland. I replied "No, Your Majesty". She asked me about so many other things and I could only smile and say "Yes, Your Majesty" with excitement. I felt that Her Majesty's kindness was immense and immeasurable.

It was one of the most impressive moments of my life, and so far nothing has compared to it since. I would have never dreamed that I would get such an honour to be so close to Her Majesty. It was my greatest reward for doing good for my country and it will stay in my heart forever as my inspiration to carry on doing more for Thai society abroad.

Minister Counselor Siriporn Panupong

I met the Minister Counselor for the first time at Thai temple, when she was the visiting mobile embassy from Sweden. She had come to offer her assistance and issue important documents to Thais in Finland, so that Thais living in Finland would not have to travel to the Thai embassy in Sweden to file for papers and documents, as Finland did not have a Thai embassy yet.

At that time I had made some green curry to bring to the temple and she had a chance try some. She said that my green curry was delicious, even though I had put in too little coconut milk as I didn't have enough, but she was pleased and kindly said that it wasn't too fatty.

I felt that she had a beautiful voice and was polite and beautifully dressed, as well as being very friendly. Most of all she did not show off that she had a big position as the Minister Counselor. Before she left, she made me promise that I would write her to tell her about all of the fun things that were going on in Finland.

Whenever I wrote to her, she was kind enough to write back every time. Each and every letter was full of teachings and advice, as she had been living abroad for a long time. She praised me for being a good and entertaining storyteller. When I organized the event to honour His Majesty the King in Helsinki, she provided me with all the necessary help and support until the job could be successfully completed, and I would be forever grateful for her kindness.

In 2008, my husband and I had a chance to vacation in Hungary. During that time, she had been moved to be stationed there, so she invited Pasi and me to the residence. Not wanting to bother her, I only requested to stay at her residence for one night.

At the at time, His Excellency the Ambassador Adisak Panupong who was stationed in Vienna, Austria, was kind enough to drive from Vienna to Hungary to come and meet me and Pasi along with his wife.

The next day, the both of them came to pick up Pasi and I from Hotel Victoria to go and stay at their residence. When I thanked them for their kindness, since they could have sent the driver, His Excellency told me something I would never forget: he said that as a civil servant who was serving the country, he was happy to assist me in any way that I needed in order to thank me for working to spread Thai culture abroad. He even praised me in front of Pasi.

I felt that for a Thai person living abroad like me, I was so lucky to have such generous civil servants like His Excellency and Her Excellency providing me guidance and support and encouraging us to work for our country in our foreign community.

On national television

When I returned to Finland, I found that my audience with Her Royal Highness had been televised on national television during the royal news segment in Thailand. My friends and family all got to watch it and they were so proud of me. One week later, I got a letter of thanks from the Bureau of the Royal Household and a certificate of my donation towards the Royal Project, as well as beautiful photograph of my meeting with the princess. P' Daeng from Turku also videotaped the segment of the news and sent it me.

I watched it with a smile on my face all day, beaming with pride. I even asked Pasi to come and watch it with me. He watched it and stroked my head while saying, *"I am so proud of you. You managed to do what I never thought would be possible"*. I replied, *"I would never see this day without you by my side to give me moral support."*

I really believe that doing good will come back to you. My family and I are living proof of this to this day.

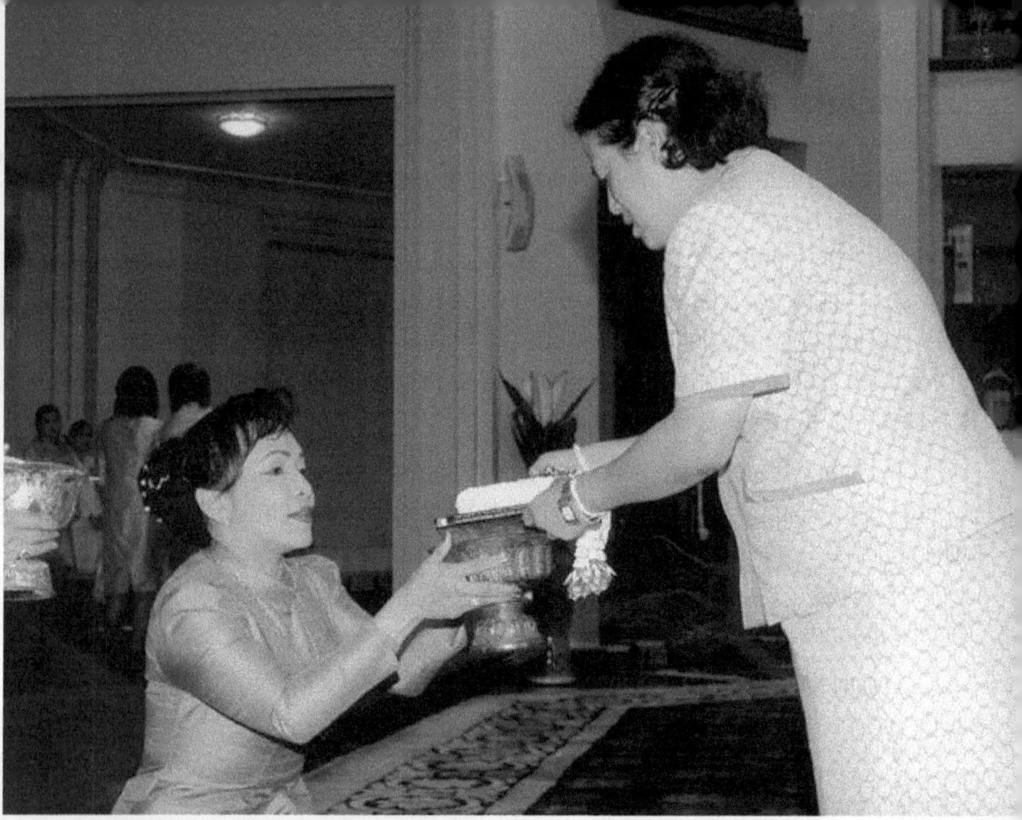

138 The Foreign In-Law สะใภ้ต่างแดน

Chapter 8
The Best of the town

As a Thai Chef

I never thought that I would end up working as a Thai chef in this lifetime, especially at a Thai restaurant abroad. Most outsiders would probably think that being a chef is easy, just a matter of finding a few good recipes or a few good cookbooks, and you're off to a good start to becoming a chef.

I can tell you from my experience working in Thai restaurants that anyone who can be a successful chef has to go through all the processes of cooking in a systematic way - organization, technique and all the tips and tricks that are important to know and learn. Most importantly, working as a chef abroad, you are required to follow all the strict rules of that country, and many people have to take and retake the exams before being able to pass.

Most of the successful chefs that I've met have their own techniques and their own recipes and have something unique that draws customers to their restaurant. I grew up amongst the best of the best in cooking and it could be said that I have the chef's blood in me, from my mother who owned her own restaurant, with knowledge and skills in food and nutrition. My aunt also started a famous Thai restaurant in Hat Yai, Bangkok and Chumpon. My aunt: Somjit Mahasi is the owner of Jae Lek restaurant in Hat Yai. Aunt Somjit's daughter: P' Rachaniporn is the owner if Prik Hom restaurant in Bangkok.

Another cousin of mine also owns a restaurant called Prik Hom, based in Chumpon.

All of these restaurants have received acclaim in terms of the tasty food from magazines and television shows. I absorbed the techniques and tips and tricks in seasoning food since I was young. However, being a chef in a Thai restaurant requires not just skill in that. The most important thing is to learn from the customers and modifying the cooking techniques to use in the right situation.

My technique

From my family, I learned the tricks of the trade from my ancestors, which has been invaluable. Combining it and using it in the appropriate situation, for example, customers who have different tastes and adapting the recipes to suit to the weather and the customers. It drives me to find new knowledge and to find the secret recipe that is loved by the customers.

Working quickly with your hands as well as with your brain is not an easy thing. Every day, the customer orders different things and in Europe, the ordering style is not similar toThailand. When the customer arrives, they would order appetizers, such as soup, spring roll, chicken satay or various spicy salads. When the appetizers are done, they will start to have rice, accompanied by a curry or another dish. Afterwards, they will round off with dessert or ice-cream. The most popular desserts are ice-cream or banana fritters, or I might suggest some Thai desserts like Bua Loi, sticky rice or banana in coconut milk, which foreigners like to try.

The heart of the restaurant is the coordination between the waitress, who takes one set of orders and reports to the chef how many are at the table and what appetizers they ordered. The chef makes the appetizers first and the waitress has to keep a watch on the guests. When the appetizers are nearly done, they report to the chef to immediately start making the second course. The rice with curry or stir-fry must be served without skipping a beat. If the guest has to wait for the second course, they will be displeased and that will mean that the restaurant is not working systematically. Just like us, when we are eating and the flow of food stops, it does not taste as good when it arrives afterwards. Another thing that is important is that the service must be completely right. Whatever the customer orders, the customer gets. You absolutely cannot get it wrong.

It's common knowledge that Thai people's eating habits are not that complicated. When we order food, we usually share all the dishes, tasting a little bit of this and a little bit of that to get a variety of flavours. With Thai food, it does not matter what comes first or last, we can all eat each other's dishes. This is not the same in Europe or America, where everyone has their own dishes and will not dare to go into another persons' dish to taste their food, with the exception of some groups that have Asian wives where they may share their dishes and will say *"It's good that we get to try a lot of things"*.

I was fortunate to start being a chef in a Thai-Chinese restaurant owned by a Chinese person, so I had the chance to learn about the tricks and tips of cooking Chinese food and I combined it with cooking Thai food, like marinating the meat, cooking with speed, improvising with ingredients and seasonings. The benefit all lies with the consumers, who get sgreat tasting food.

Every time a customer is satisfied with the food that I made, I would feel proud and full of happiness for helping to make Thai food well-known all over the world. As for the tips in cooking, I had a motto that a foreigner should taste Thai food exactly as it is. It should not need any extra seasoning, and lastly:

1. Thai food has to be colourful.
2. It has to smell good.
3. It has to taste good. These are the teachings that my mother constantly taught me.

An old story

Before becoming a chef based on a friend's recommendation, I used to be a sous-chef in a Thai restaurant with a Chinese chef, which had me a little puzzled, but I didn't dare say that I was a chef, because I was just filling in for a friend. I was chopping up vegetables and the staff could not stop watching me, since I was very good at slicing and dicing. My speed was second to none and I have made many guys embarrassed by my skills before.

Back at that job as a sous-chef, when I went home I could hardly sleep. The image of that chef cooking for Finns was embedded in my mind and bothered me so much that I had to ask myself why was I so stressed out. It wasn't my restaurant and I was only a temporary staff. But the image of the green curry with milk instead of coconut milk and curry paste that wasn't green curry paste, followed by onions and canned mushrooms nearly drove me insane.

On the second day, I would be astounded by a Pad Thai made with ketchup and sweet chilli sauce, as well as cabbage and paprika peppers to add colour to the dish. I couldn't see how the dish could be a Pad Thai, and when I tasted it, I nearly spat it out because I could taste nothing but sweetness.

In the afternoon, the customers ordered Chicken and Cashew Nuts and I waited to see what the chef would do. I saw that he did not fry the chicken and stir-fried the dish until it was completely black. The canned mushrooms and canned bamboo shoots followed. It was finished with cashew nuts. I touched the pan, the dish was so salty that I nearly walked out of the kitchen because I couldn't stand it.

I told the owner that this wasn't Thai food. Anyone can run a Thai food business wherever they are from, but the most important thing is to have true knowledge or hire a cook who has knowledge in the food you are hoping to make a business out of. It can't be done casually, with the loss lying with the consumer. Running a business selfishly simply taking advantage of the good name of Thai food can never make a successful business.

Finnish people or even other people around the world may have never tasted Thai food, but with advanced technology, they can look up Thai food, the way of cooking it, and the recipe on the Internet. Making anything that is looks like Thai food but tastes nothing like it is like cheating the customer.

The restaurant owner became very angry and said he had no problem finding a Thai cook. After that day, I never set foot in that place again. I found out later that they used to have a Thai cook, but the Chinese had a plan to learn the recipes and start making the food themselves. When they were confident enough, they forced the Thai cook to leave. I was sure that sneaking around trying to learn the recipe must be confusing. They might have gotten confused until the food would not even be good enough to be called dog food.

Now, that restaurant has closed down. I suspect that the restaurant owner might have gone to hang himself or been demoted to a line cook in some other restaurant. But what I know for sure is that Finns are better off now not having to eat fake Thai food anymore in that place.

Taste

Making food from any country carries its own unique characteristics of that country as well as the taste of the cook. No matter how skilled they are, if they are not familiar with the taste of that food, even if it is exactly as the recipe says, you will feel that it is not right. Is it the wrong recipe? No. Does it taste strange? No. But what it is lacking is what Thai people call the taste of the cook's hand.

It would be the same if I went to cook Italian, Chinese or Japanese food. No matter how accurately I follow the recipe, the missing thing is smell, colour, taste and the right feeling that is in the dish since before time.

Every dish from every country has a history. Thai food has been around since the old days until the present. It has been adapted, tried and tested until cookbooks were made, resulting in millions in earnings.

But, not every cookbook is of great quality and everyone trusts different recipes. Everyone has their own recipe. Even if the writer is a good cook and the ingredients weighed up, every step followed and reproduced, the results that comes out could never be the same as the owner of the recipe.

That is because the cook's hand is different. The context, the place, and many other factors are also different. That is no great matter. As long as you follow the recipe, you can cook and taste authentic Thai food according to your personal taste.

Buffet food

When I was hired to be responsible for making buffet food, it was one of the most valuable experiences. Making buffet food is not difficult and isn't easy at the same time. The heart of it is to estimate the volume of the food corectly, and to work quickly.

Making buffet food has to be made in a large quantity, with many dishes on the go at the same time. You have to take care of 3-4 dishes at once, as well as control the time that you spend on each dish accordingly.

Even more than that, you have to carefully monitor the dishes that are running out in order to make more in due time. As well as that, you have to change the container regularly so that it looks neat. Another important thing is to set out the food to look beautiful and presentable and inviting at the same time.

The buffet culture of Finland or Europeans is to take enough food for yourself and take more after it is finished. Everyone finishes all of their food.

I experienced this for myself when I go out to eat with my husband's family and my friends. They see the value in food and finish all of the food on their plate. They do not put that much food on each plate but everyone seems to be okay with this.

In a Finn visit, the highlight is not the food that you use to entertain your guests, but the exchange and conversation. On the contrary, in Thailand, when we are entertaining guests, everything seems so chaotic and full of too many courtesies, for example, the food has to be beautiful, elegantly presented, and there must be many things to choose from. For this reason, in every visit, everyone pays attention to the food that is being used to entertain the guests. Anyone that uses bad food or puts out a small quality of food for the guests will get badmouthed. I think that those people should cook for themselves at home and stay alone, rather than going out to eat at other people's homes and gossip about the hosts.

Giving thanks

A great reward that I always get from working at the restaurant is the customer's thanks. In the beginning, I was surprised every time I heard them giving thanks before walking out of the restaurant, because I was used to Thailand, where the restaurant owner and service staff have to bow or greet the customers as they leave the restaurant.

I was honoured and pleased every time I heard thanks, because it showed that the customers were satisfied with the service that they get. I also felt that expressing thanks is a culture that shows politeness and respect for the other profession.

At the same time, I think that the Thai attitude is too deferent towards the customer, since we think that the customer is bringing us revenue. Sometimes, this has a negative impact, the customers are usually carried away and think that they are the most important people, because they hold the money, to the point that they are rude to waiters.

Thai society should take a look at some of the countries in Europe, for example Finland, everyone is honored according to what they do, without the rule that the customer is always the one that deserves respect.

Setting up "Tamarind" Thai restaurant

When I worked in a Thai restaurant with a Chinese owner, I had a chance to create a masterpiece. I helped to set up **"Tamarind"** Thai restaurant. I suggested to my boss, *"If you want to create a Thai restaurant that is reputable, you have to have a Thai chef and Thai waitresses who understand the details of the food and can suggest items from the menu and ingredients to the customers."*

Luckily, my boss was accepting and trusted me to handle the procedures, from making the menu to decorating the restaurant. I went back to Thailand to buy decorations and Thai products, such as plates and bowls that I selected myself, choosing Thai celadon, a lacquered pottery which is very famous in Thailand. I chose decorative pieces that had a uniquely Thai look that they could never see anywhere else apart from at Tamarind. Some customers were so impressed they asked to buy the utensils from the shop, which made me as the buyer very proud.

"Tamarind" was such a huge success that my boss opened 4 more branches and hired chefs from Thailand to serve up authentic, tasty Thai food. I was happy for my boss and for the success of "Tamarind" and was inspired to open my own Thai restaurant later.

My own restaurant business

Even though I was determined to start my own restaurant business, the procedures for doing business abroad is no easy feat with everything from registration, obtaining licenses, etc. I had to start from zero again.

If I did not have support from all of my friends and acquaintances, especially Pasi, this project would have been over even before it began. Actually, Pasi was supportive morally and financially. With Pasi as my investor, I was the proud owner of my own restaurant.

As for the details of the management and proceedings that could get the business started, I had to do that all myself. I could not get anyone to help me because in a foreign community, everyone has their own obligations.

During that time, my friends nicknamed me *"Ms. Frizzy"*, running around doing all my errands until my hair was frizzy. I never got to take care of myself. I had to photograph the food, make stickers, find kitchen utensils and kitchen equipment. I had a great personal assistant, which was Pasi of course, advising me and studying all the rules and regulations of the restaurant business in Finland, which has to be obeyed by every single establishment. The documents, safety, cleanliness, temperature of the food and many other details had to be followed strictly.

I happily followed all the rules and guidance because it was the only way that I could be sure that all of my staff and all of my customers would be in a safe and hygienic environment. The business started off with a lot of excitement and was well-supported by customers who were excited to try the taste of real Thai food at an affordable price.

Tired days

I woke up with a startle, not knowing when I had fallen asleep. I was on the way home on the bus and when I looked outside the window, I was surprised by not seeing any familiar landmarks. I thought to myself that *"I must have come a long way from home."* When I thought that, I got up to ask the driver where I was, and when I got my reply, I quickly got off the bus. At that time the temperature was freezing and it was snowing heavily. It was dark all around me.

At that time, I could feel the loneliness and fear creeping in. In actual fact, Finland is one of the safest countries in the world, but I could not help being scared due to the darkness and the unfamiliar surroundings. I waited for the bus to come to take me home.

I thought to myself that if I kept falling asleep so often, it would not be a good thing. When I looked back on that person, I pitied myself. Most people probably thought I lived a comfortable life abroad, however, the fact was, I was working harder than I was working in Thailand.

Being a chef is already hard work as it is, but being a restaurant owner on top of that is multiplying the responsibilities - managing the finances, placing food orders and goods, and finding new ways for the restaurant to stay open without making losses. Lastly, when I got home, before I went to bed, I couldn't help but wonder whether I would have customers tomorrow, whether I would have rent at the end of the month, and whether I would have enough money to pay wages.

The other person in as much stress as me is my restaurant's financial sponsor, Pasi. If the restaurant business went well, his wife would be more tired and he and the children would not get to see me much. If the restaurant business failed, the burden would fall on Pasi because he would lose his investment. I never got a good night's sleep. The physical tiredness was coupled with mental tiredness until my body could not take it anymore and I accidentally fell asleep. When I got home, I had to make food for my husband and children, clean the house, do the dishes, and by the time I went to bed I was exhausted. When I was younger, I remembered that every morning before dawn at 3 a.m., my parents would wake up to make food and desserts to sell in the morning at 6 a.m. Customers would already be standing at the front of the shop, waiting.

They were there to buy the food and sell it on. Every day there would be customers from all walks of life, whether it was schools, factories, the army barracks, hospitals, etc. That was the busiest time which me, my brother and sister would have to get up and help out before going to school. Sometimes we would fall asleep while going to school and my teacher would throw chalk at me. I remember that when I was younger, all of us three would have to help out with chores. Nobody had the time to go and play like other children.

After school, all three of us already had jobs waiting for us. Everyone knew their own job, especially my brother, who had to carry out more of the chores than everyone else. My brother was the responsible one who would finish all the jobs my mother assigned for him.

Sometimes, if a mistake occurred, my mother would get cross and in a bad mood. I would often see my brother crying, but we were all happy to help out our parents, seeing that our parents worked much harder than us. However, that was a long time ago and when we were younger, we had a lot of energy to dedicate to many tasks, which were suitable for children. That is a far cry from today, when I am much older and my body is old and tired, and I could not do a job which required me to stand up for many hours at a time anymore. I had no choice, however, since I decided to go into business without listening to Pasi's protests. I had to grit my teeth and carry on no matter how tired I was. I was dedicated to the success of the restaurant which I helped to build with my own hands. Seeing an empty space come alive and become a popular spot, with long lines of customers queuing up to buy food was enough to put me in a good mood. I was so proud of not letting Pasi down and wasting his money.

My customers

My restaurant *"Prik Hom"* was such a success and was so highly praised by my customers, who called it *"The Best of the Town."* I felt that this was the highest honour and the best prize that I could get from opening my own restaurant. My determination to fight against the obstacles was not in vain and my determination to make delicious Thai food for my foreign customers was very well received.

My success came at a prize though. Every day, I hardly had any time for my family. Pasi and the children had to wait for me to finish my duties at the restaurant before being able to go back to take care of them. My clean and tidy house became a mess. At that time I felt that the happiness I had in my family had vanished. When someone offered to buy my restaurant, I immediately agreed without hesitation. Even though a lot of people felt sorry that I was selling the business at its peak, for me, nothing was more valuable or more important than my family.

Even now, the only thing that I regret and still think about since I stopped my restaurant business is my relationship with the customers because I gave importance to all of the customers who came to my restaurants and treated them like friends. The service that I gave to my customers every time is not only to serve food and collect money. I cared about the details, even how they feel towards the food and the service. If there are small children, I would help to take care of the little ones while the parents eat. The customers were impressed and quite a lot of them became my friends.

Even now when I've sold the restaurant, a lot of customers still call to wish me happy New Year and Merry Christmas. A lot of them call me to ask me about my news and a lot of them that I meet by accident could only complain that they miss having good quality Thai food by Khun Porntipa. Some of them saw my news in the newspaper and still followed me to my new workplace, which made me so grateful. I would like to take this opportunity to thank all of my dear customers from the bottom of my heart.

Chapter 9
Happy days

My youth

I grew up in the countryside and studied at Ban Klong Wa school, which was opposite my house and reachable within 10 steps. There was no hardship in my childhood, since I was born into a family that sold food and sweets. Therefore, my livelihood was a lot better than a lot of other families that lived nearby.

At the same time, my parents instilled in us the habit of working to help the family. We did not get the chance to go out or do other activities like other families did, since we had to help out at home. As for education, my parents encouraged us to study as much as possible. They were prepared to do everything in order to make sure that the family was well-off and as comfortable as anyone else.

The house that I lived in when I was younger was a single storey wooden house. The back of the house was an extension made of corrugated iron for cooking and making desserts. There was a well in the kitchen and we pulled up water through this well, which was convenient. The back of the house was a forest grove where you could hunt small animals like rabbits and birds. I had my bow and arrow and fun on my own when my parents were not home.

The neighbourhood kids loved to call me out to play because every time I did, I would be armed with a bunch of desserts to give to my friends. My mother often noticed that the desserts were missing and knew that there could be no other offender but me, and I would often get scolded. Still, the sweets carried on going missing until she got tired of complaining. She felt sorry for me for not being able to go out anywhere but the forest behind our house, and for the friends that I had, who had to be lured by sweets to play with me.

When I was a teenager, I had a string of unruly adventures. I loved to take the motorcycle out to the waterfalls or go to the beach with my friends. Sometimes I would get a spanking for this as my parents were scared that I would get into an accident with a lorry, or drown.

Both of my elder siblings, in comparison, were well behaved and did whatever they were told, which made my parents very relieved. I was loved by both of them, perhaps more so since I was the youngest, and especially by my father, which meant that I had a big ego listening less to his teachings. Even when I was a teenager, I did not have a lot of freedom and had to stay within the rules of our house.

Sometimes I wondered why my family was not as free as other families. I asked my mother once I had started a family of my own, and she replied that since my parents had to work hard, if there were no rules, how could we be disciplined? My parents had less time to groom us and to keep a close eye on us. Without those rules, we could have ended up anywhere. These were reasons that I agreed with and I immediately understood the love and care they gave to me as parents.

Back then I did not understand and could only think that my parents were strict and that meant that they scolded us all the time and didn't love us. Even when I have grown up, I can still remember the days of my youth and I think that the way my parents disciplined us all to be responsible young adults by making us help them since we were young, meant that all of us grew up with strength, perseverance and determination. We never give up in the face of obstacles and never complain about hard work.

My family was often praised by the school teachers and neighbours, saying that the son of this family is very diligent and helps his parents with work, as well as having good academic grades and getting scholarships throughout.

When my brother finished his studies, he always sent money to my parents. As for the girls, I often heard them say that we were very hardworking, as well as being charming and polite. The latter quality was definitely not me. They probably meant my sister, since everyone knew that I didn't have very good manners and my rebelliousness was my trademark. Whatever my parents taught me, I always had a good reason not to listen, therefore none of the neighbourhood boys ever looked twice at me and they were definitely not interested in making me their wife.

My sister, however, was the belle of the village to other parents, who were impressed with her beauty, her hardworking ways, and how obedient she was. I could only agree with this observation.

Even now, my sister is still very polite and good-mannered. She is a great mother, raising her two children by herself as her husband is a civil servant and has to be stationed in the provinces. It has been this way in her marriage ever since she got married until now, 28 years later.

Not only is she a great mother, she also has a job at the Electrical Generating Authority of Thailand, which is not at all easy to do while raising two children. But her children are growing up nicely and have great jobs and great manners, having been taught well by their mother, who in turn was taught by my parents.

These things let me know how valuable the teachings of a mother and father can be towards the way you live in the future. I was not surprised to know that both my brother and sister are very successful in their lives. Looking back at myself, I realized that my disobedience and not listening to my parent's teachings made me live an incomplete life and I had to endure a lot of hardship and weather a lot of storms in my life.

However, due to my strength and the knowledge that was given to me by example by my parents, as well as having a loving family to support me, I was able to get through many storms. Now, I carry with me all of their teachings, to use from now and in the future.

These are the most valuable things that I got from my family, who are role models for me and have been a guiding force for me, contributing to my success today.

The willingness to learn

In many of the things in life, many things add up together to make sure that we survive, and one of those things is the willingness to learn.

When I was younger, I wanted to learn how to make clothes, but I was too young and I was still in school. My interest inspired me to buy old clothes to mend and draw out patterns on a piece of paper and find scraps of cloth to make it. At home we had a Singer sewing machine, when I finished my work, my mother was astonished and my father was so pleased. After that, I started making my own clothes, and when I finished high school, my father allowed me to go to dressmaking school, just like I wanted.

While I was studying there, I was interested in makeup, hairdressing and I sneaked off to go and study it. My friend, who was a makeup artist in a film crew invited me to go and study makeup artistry and I got the opportunity to work with the crew quite often.

When I returned home, my mother had set up a new business selling readymade clothes. I was the tailor at her store and also the sales person at the same time. However, I was still curious to know more. I wanted to know how to paint clothes and make tie-dye and batik. I applied to study home economics and I saw all the different departments like artificial flowers, hand woven crafts, cross stitching, carving, necklace making, pottery making. I made it my mission to study all of these things at the same time and my mother used to say I was at risk of drowning in too much knowledge.

These subjects helped to build up a love for the arts and I was enthusiastic about all of the things that I created. I was happy every time I got to do creative things. Due to my brother going abroad to study for his Masters degree in America which required a lot of money, I decided to help my mother with the family's business for three years, but it wasn't enough. My parents got frustrated with me knowing too much and not wanting to stay at home.

After the shop closed, I would find the chance to take extra jobs since I was bored of selling, which was the same day in, day out.

A lot of times, I had to travel upcountry to put on bridal makeup, which is the thing that I liked most about those jobs. I loved going far way up country, seeing different things, seeing the cultures of the local people where they help each other fell a cow, pigs, chicken, to use as offerings, cooking them in big pots and pans, the fun and entertaining wedding procession with unlimited food and drinks. At the same time, I was being made to feel so welcomed.

Some of the children would crowd around to look at my clothes and shoes since I was following the latest fashion due to my family running a boutique. It might look a little funny dressed up like that and walking along a rice paddy field, but I didn't care about all the eyes that were watching. Everyone welcomed me and treated me like I was a superstar, which made me very pleased.

The host would entertain us without reservation until I hardly wanted to go home. I told my parents that I would be home by evening, but my parents still had no clue where I was after three days, which often made my parents angry. I was happy with being with those people, living a different lifestyle, being attended to by the country boys, many of whom would look at me with gooey eyes as if I was some kind of angel.

When it was time for me to go home, they would make sad puppy dog eyes that their angel was leaving. They probably didn't know that after three days I would become the devil. Nobody there knew what I was truly like. I was an average looking young girl with a lot of craziness in me.

Back then, I used to ride a motorcycle with more than ten of my friends into the graveyard and whenever anyone was caught off their guard, I would pull out their keys and ride away. Anyone who got that treatment would be scared out of their wits.

Many of my friend's parents would be sick of these crazy ideas, which could be fatal if anyone of them would go into shock. Whenever we meet up now, I would get called out for this until I was ashamed sometimes and I don't know how I thought about something like that.

I could go on for days about my wild streaks, but I dare not reveal all of them, fearing that my kids and Pasi will just abandon me. That was a long time ago, but it serves as a good memory about my curiosity, which has led me through many good and bad, and refreshing experiences.

My mother's inheritance

Out of the three of us, I am probably the one who has been through the most hardship and adventures. However, through all of these experiences, I have managed to survive and make it through. My mother used to say *"The willingness to learn will be your path to success"* and I have used this throughout my entire life to know that it is absolutely true.

Most importantly, my mother has been a great role model and conveyed all the best things to all of her children. I am the closest to my parents and they have tried to teach me to be independent since I was a child. My mother taught me everything including housework and the restaurant business. I am lucky to have such a talented mother.

My mother told me that long ago, when Thailand had no cooking school or bakery schools, and even if they did she could not afford to go because she was too poor, she walked past a Thai sweet shop, selling Thai sweets such as Mor Gaeng, Thong Yip, Thong Yod, and she wanted to know how to make it so that she could make it as a career. She walked into the shop and applied for a job so that she could learn the skills, but they declined as they already had staff.

She told the owner that she didn't want payment, she will work for free to learn their trade. The answer was still no, since they were careful of letting people know their secrets, in case someone opened up a place to compete with them.

My mother approached this shop every day until the owner relented and allowed her to work there, but they did not teach her everything straightaway. She had to do everything they asked her to, while keeping a close eye all the time and noting down everything when she got home. After many months when she learned everything and became skilled, she started looking for a way to make sweets to sell. She started with selling one thing a day, gradually adding one more until the table was full. That is how my mother's business started, from small to big, like a stepladder. It could be said that my mother is a cautious investor. She only ventured out to selling goods with the hope of making a strong basis for her family and she was successful, managing to send us all to get good education.

I can safely say that all of us grew up thanks to her vocational skills. My mother has tirelessly worked through until she could provide for the family. Even though she didn't have a good education, she persevered until she succeeded and has seen all of us succeed in our lives.

Changing the reader

As I mentioned in the beginning, I have loved reading since I was young. The person who gave me the inspiration and encouraged me to read is my mother. My mother read everything, from magazines, novels, history, politics, Buddhist teachings and Thai cooking.

Her favourite books are the series of historical novel called Conqueror of Ten Directions by Jacob, which spoke of Thai-Burmese relations when Ayudhaya fell to the Burmese army. The Thai soldiers had to send a prince and princess as hostages to Hongsawadee, Burma.

My mother could recall the whole story scene by scene, as well as remember all of the character's names. I also read it but didn't absorb it or remember every character as well as my mother. It was surprising though, that my reading time had to be done on the sly since my family had a business so none of us had much time to read novels. But I was always the one to break the rules. If my mother forbade anything, it was a safe bet that she would see it happening soon enough. Actually, even though my mother was busy, she always had enough time to read. She never stopped me from reading, but she usually told me to read my school books instead.

After I returned from school, my mother would have me tending to the restaurant so that she could go home to rest. I wouldn't hesitate to go to my regular bookshop, borrow the books and hide them away, waiting for the time when there were no customers when I could sit in peace and read. Customers who came to the shop would have to yell out loudly to me to get my attention, so my mother complained every time she found the books that were hidden away.

She only complained for the sake of it though. After that, she would come and ask to borrow some of them from me. I couldn't resist teasing her. However, I understood that she is tired and wants to use books as an escape from stress and tiredness.

At that time, my mother and I were reading all the same books, and she told me that reading could change a person.

Now, I understand that it is true. My mother always had wise words to teach us, with many examples and many stories, sometimes poems or idioms that could be used as a lesson. It was because she loved reading that could do that and she always had something good to teach us.

I only realized the change within myself when I read more. I started to be able to analyze and search for information, teaching myself from books and my environment, from past to present.

Reading helped me to learn and to be enlightened without being influenced. These things are very useful to me and I am incredibly fortunate to have my parents guiding and teaching me.

Not only have my parents given me knowledge, they also gave me a great life, a great livelihood, protecting me, taking care of me. These things are more valuable than the greatest wealth. I will treasure it forever and teach my children and grandchildren how hardworking their grandparents were and what a great example they set.

5 years of loneliness

After I left home despite my parent's protestations, the first thing I had to face was fear, being alone in a square room with just a bed and a closet. On the first night, I was terrified and tried to close my eyes to sleep to be able to go to work the next day. I had gotten a singing job, took a look at a place to rent, and then asked for my mother's permission. My mother was furious. She said that I had already done everything before I asked for permission, as if I did not have any respect for her. My reason was, if I had asked for permission without a job or a place to live, she would just be worried and she would not let me leave home. However, we understood different things.

On the first day of the job, I was very excited to meet singers and other friends of the same profession. The payment was very little for a new young singer.

After three months, I found a new job at a new place with better pay. My work ran smoothly. That is, I went to work at 7 p.m. and clocked out at midnight. I sang Thai, International and Chinese songs.

I started to feel that life was too ordinary. That's why I went to apply for work at night clubs, which I felt was more exciting. That is, I got a chance to sing songs from all genres and got to sing with all of the other singers. The music continued for two hours.

Every singer has their own order of when they have to go onstage. We had to remember the preceding singer very well, like a medley. The dancers also must not miss a beat. I was enjoying my new job a lot because I got to wear glittery dresses every day, that's what I loved most about my job.

My father came to watch me work once, but he said that it was too loud and too crowded. He liked places that were light and airy. When I was singing, he would smile at me and look on admiringly, then afterwards make suggestions about which songs I should sing.

My father used to suggest which songs were suitable or unsuitable for my voice and I always tried to follow his advice. I have been singing his songs ever since, even until now.

In the latter years, I would be contacted to sing in Bangkok, usually in hotels, which already have accommodation there. It was more convenient since I could bargain and also had a little bit more experience. Even though my salary was rising, you can rest assured the hotel's owners were making the maximum use of me.

I had to come downstairs and sing during the lunch hour between 11 a.m. until 2 p.m. After that, I had 2 hours to sleep and then I had to get dressed for the evening round between 8 p.m. and midnight, alternating between the cocktail lounge and restaurant. After midnight I went down to sing at the nightclub. Every other singer was running around, as busy as me.

For me, the job was harder than most since I had promised my friends at the pub that I would help them out after work. It wasn't too far from where I was staying so when the night club closed at 2 a.m., I rushed to change my clothes into the rocker look to suit the atmosphere of folk music. I was at my happiest when I was singing Thai folk music and hanging out with the old people who loved to talk about democracy and reminisce about old times on October 1976 and 14 October, where the ashes were still smoldering constantly.

The song lyrics were usually from those who had survived the jungle after hiding there for years. The atmosphere was electric. Some people would sing along with the music and after work, we would reminisce about the past, remember the brave ones, and those who were brutally killed on the coup on 6 December 1976.

During the first year, I was not surprised why I had the strength and never got tired at work. I had many friends who shared the same spirit who would motivate me to go on. I never got a single payment from my friend but I would get recommendations from those who had followed me from the nightclub. Everyone was taken in by the atmosphere, which was different from the place they had just left.

Most of the customers were teachers, lawyers, researchers, and were pleased to be our regular customers. But there is another type of customers that I did not dare ask to come along, and those are the businessmen or high-level government officials. Some of those people liked to come during the lunch hour… to come and have lunch and drink until the afternoon. No one made a move to get back to work. I used to ask them whether they would be going back to work, and their answer was that they could go to work whenever they wanted because they were in high-level positions and did not have to fear anybody.

The second time is during the night, when there would be drinkers and dance partners. Those who were high and mighty would order a lot of girls to come and sit with them to feel superior to the next table. They would keep tabs and pay at the end of the month, or sometimes they would not pay and the hotel owner would not dare to ask, for fear of their influences. Most of the time, I knew that they did not pay. That is the system in Thailand. Some of them were old enough to be my father but would hire girls who were young enough to be their daughter. I felt pity for those men when I heard the girls complain that those men are old enough to be dead and were boring as death itself. Whenever they got drunk, their hands would start crawling. Thus was the nightlife. On the other hand though, there are many government officials who are honest, faithful to their duties and are responsible to their families.

The cops and soldiers on border patrol working in danger in the midst of the terrorists are the most special. I salute those men, giving up their lives for the country. Sadly, some of the top level government officials go out drinking, eating and being merry while the low-level officials are out on the border walking through the jungle and living their life in the middle of danger. They never see the night lights or get to hold beautiful girls with pale skin. The only thing they can do is hold on to their guns and protect their country.

The music with fierce and aggressive beat

In case you're wondering what beat that is about, let me preface this story by saying that I was contacted to sing in the southern border provinces close to Malaysia. At that time I felt tied down to my old job, shuttling between night and day without any time for rest. My body was on the verge of collapse and I had dark circles under my eyes which required many layers of concealer to hide them.

After I took off my makeup, I would look at myself and the image would stare back at me with pity. Would my parents have any idea that their once-cheerful daughter has withered away until they would hardly recognize me anymore? So, I accepted the offer to go and work somewhere else.

The new workplace was a modern hotel with a foreign boss. He was nice, kind and fiercely handsome with a very stern wife who was beautiful like a superstar. I really liked her and she really liked me. We became good friends. A lot of the time, she would come and stay with me in my hotel room to catch her flirtatious husband in the act and see if he was bringing girls back to the hotel. I became a detective. Every time she caught her husband cheating, she came crying to my room until I hardly got any sleep. After she vented and told me all of her sorrows, she went back to sleep but I had to go and sing without getting a wink of sleep. I couldn't quite understand why the boss's indiscretions had to affect a lowly employee like me.

At my new job, there was a mix of customers. Most of the business was focused on foreigners, and I was not required to sing during the lunch hour. My job started at 9 p.m. at the night club and went on until 2 a.m. The accommodation was in the hotel itself, which offered me a lot of convenience and safety with 3 free meals. The atmosphere of the night club was different from night clubs in Bangkok or other places, since 80% of the guests were Malaysian and hence the beat was required to be "fierce and aggressive", which is the way that Malaysians dance. It was hugely popular with the dancers and the girls had to learn the right way to dance along with the beat.

I went along to learn too because I wanted to try the beautiful and exotic dance moves. When I sang and danced along at the same time, I attracted a lot of attention. Some of the customers were impressed and gave me huge tips. I thought to myself that the effort to learn this dance was completely paying off. I was in love with my new job since it was a great change of atmosphere and musical style. I started to sing Malaysian and Chinese songs, which made me feel great since I personally liked Chinese music.

I sang those songs without knowing the meaning of the words, but tried to sound as much like I knew what I was singing as possible. The challenging thing is that I had to work very hard, picking out the words and verses. I had a personal rule that I would never have lyric sheets on the stage (which was the golden rule at the school I used studied at).

Sometimes, I reconsidered having a sheet because I saw other people do it and I was tempted to be lazy and get more sleep, but I became unconfident on stage while my eyes were focused on the song sheet and couldn't dance the way I wanted to. I felt unprofessional and felt like I was not deserving of my salary, so after that I never used lyric sheets again.

If I was not confident that I could remember the lyrics, I would not sing the song. Nobody could force me and I could design the set list that I wanted to sing without the boss's interference. I worked there happily for 8 months before receiving the terrible news that my father had been hit by a car and was in intensive care. I quickly rushed to be by my father's side, fearing that he would be leaving me, leaving us.

When my father left the ICU and was transferred to the care of a normal ward, I regained some confidence and I was sure that he was past the critical point. He wrote me a message on a piece of paper telling me to go back to work and not to worry about him, that he would be okay. I reluctantly went back to work because I could not miss work on Fridays and Saturdays due to hotel regulations, a fact that my father knew very well.

I had planned that after I finished singing on Saturday, I would come back to stay with my father for 3-4 days but while I was singing on Saturday night, I couldn't sing due to feeling extremely anxious.

Back at work, I sang the wrong lyrics on stage, which I had never done before, until my band leader had to ask me what was wrong. I replied that I didn't know, but my heart was beating so fast, as if I had never been on stage before. My hands were shaking and I felt nervous until I couldn't stand it anymore. I decided to go up to my room to call my father at the hospital.

The reply came back that my father had died two hours ago. I clutched the telephone and asked the nurse in a whisper to double check since she may have mixed up the names. When the answer was final, my heart shattered and I had no more energy to sing. I couldn't even go home straightaway because by that time, it was so late and there were no more buses running. I waited for the morning to come. It was the most torture I had ever felt in my life. I lay awake in the room, praying for my father to come to me. I missed him very badly. I regretted not being able to say goodbye and not being able to see him one last time.

I knew that my father wanted to see me before he died because he loved me the most, but I didn't get the chance to do that for him. I felt so much regret and blamed myself for being at work. If I hadn't come back to work, I would be able to take care of him before he died. How could I have forgotten that the distance from home to my workplace was 4 hours of travelling? Those important lessons taught me never to let time go to waste. If I think I could do something, I do it straightaway. I don't want to wait until tomorrow, fearing that it would be too late. Nowadays, whenever I think of my father, I always cry and Pasi and the kids would have to come and console me. I regretted the time while he was still alive and that I never had the chance to repay him. I never got to serve him or make him comfortable in his old age. I always thought that he was not that old and he still had a lot of time.

The future is so uncertain. Now, all I want to do is to achieve my goals, be able to take care of myself and take care of my family. I made a promise to myself that I would make time to go back home and take care of my mother, who is counting the days until the grandchildren and I come home to stay. Wherever I am, always think that my father is above me, watching me and loving me. I love and miss him still.

Beauties in a fish tank

You might already know what this means, so what was I doing being involved with all of those beautiful women?

18 years ago, I was invited by a friend working in a salon to go and put on makeup for the women working behind the glass. Every day, I would apply makeup on about 30-50 women. It was quite a considerable income.

I had to drive there at 8 a.m. and put on makeup on them in time for midday because in the afternoon, Malaysian customers would come to pick up the women. Putting makeup on the women was not that hard; what was harder was that they all had to be finished on time. Nothing much needed to be done, everyone had their foundation and powder applied, and I only had to do their eyebrows and eye makeup.

The thing that excited me most was seeing those women selected by the guests who came. It was like seeing a piece of pork or chicken being sold in the market. At that time, the cheerers would describe the qualities of the girls, saying whatever they could to interest the customer. I felt pity for the ones that were not chosen and had to wait for the next round. Some of them who didn't get selected blamed the makeup artist. I sat there, smiled and didn't say anything. I understood the feeling only too well. However, in the morning, that same girl would be sitting there, waiting for me to put makeup on her again.

From all of my experience meeting and being in contact with those women, everyone was in a very sorry situation. Some of them were tricked to leave home and never got the chance to go back. Some of them were lucky to meet rich men who wanted to take care of them, but they were no different than a pet.

Sometimes I would see their faces black and blue, with bruises on their bodies. When I asked, they said that the customers raped them. They couldn't complain or go to the police because they didn't want to have problems with the owner.

I was sympathetic and understanding to those women more than anyone since I was their Agony Aunt during the time I was putting makeup on them. Sometimes, I had to apply makeup and cry along with them at the same time. I was trusted by those beauties and thus I would get to hear stories that I never thought I would hear or never thought could exist in this world.

It was like a tale of different lives. I was saddened and moved by all of those women. I secretly wondered that whether I would have their patience if I had to live in the conditions that they lived in.

Not only did I get to put makeup on the girls, I had the chance to be makeup artist for the stars, models and high society. I found that the life of those in high society were no different than those in the glass cage at all.

People's lives are different. Some of the stars I worked with have been taken advantage of by producers and managers to get to where they are. How many high society women are in turmoil over their husband and children? How many are suffering from losses in their business and did not dare to face the truth?

Everyone's problems and concerns gets expressed to the inner circles or to a makeup artist like me, who can be accepting of all situations and can even be an agony aunt in some situations.

These experiences taught me that everyone has different problems and they act as they see most fit. Helping other people provides comfort for me and I am happy to be an outlet for them. It helps me learn and I have used the lessons from those people to help me with my own life too.

Chapter 10
12 years in Finland and My Observations

The other side of the coin

The main problem experienced by Thai women abroad is the problem of our image. Most foreigners had a negative opinion of the Thai women living abroad. They believe that Thai women who have got married and moved abroad are those who used to work in the sex industry.

I have been spat at and called a prostitute, but I haven't minded because I thought to myself that the human heart is both good and bad depending on where it lies.

Usually, I thought that foreigners look down on Thai women because of the information that they get from the press, whether it is cinema, newspapers or magazines, or even the hearsay of the foreign friends that have holidayed in Thailand before.

I found a book in Finland where the author described the tales of the tricks and trades of Thai sex workers: how they can confess their love for many men, especially foreigners, to trick them into marrying them. The author concluded that Finn men should become wiser after reading the truths in the book. The hidden message is that Finn men should think hard before they marry Thai women!

I thought that the author is one of the examples of many people who usually judge the problem from only one side of the coin. It made all of their opinions clouded with prejudice.

In actual fact, everything in the world, whether people or things, have a positive and negative side. There is good and bad mixed in between, like a two-sided coin.

The sex workers that they look down on might have some other aspects that are nobler than many of the honourable people in society. Some of them are prostitutes working to keep their family alive. They let themselves do work that is looked down upon so that their family can live well. On the other hand, a lot of those who are wealthy and well-respected in society are corrupt and will do anything to get rich.

I have known many prostitutes who have tried to turn a new leaf and become a full time housewife after they married Finnish men, but they were beaten an abused by their husbands. Some of them were even forced to become prostitutes, while the husbands turned themselves into pimps.

In this case, the behavior of the foreigners who tricked those girls are even worse and they should be ashamed of themselves, but I have never seen a book being written about these men, just the same as there are many Thai women who have succeeded in their careers and become famous abroad but there is no book telling their story to the foreign community. The movies in Hollywood play on the issues of prostitution and drugs in Bangkok instead of saying the other good and interesting qualities that could be found in Thailand.

In my opinion, I think it depends which side of the coin you choose to look at, but most importantly, you need to acknowledge that there are two sides of the same coin and think about whether there is another side that you haven't seen. If you choose to overlook the other side, you will never open your mind and escape your prejudices.

Rights and equality in marriage

The entire time I hsve been in Finland, I have gotten to experience the European culture, which gave a lot of importance to the equality between men and women. Even the marriage law protects the balance in a Finn marriage, or even the equal help that is expected in raising a child between a husband and wife, or alternating duties in housework.

This is in contrast to most countries in Asia, especially Thailand, where the man is still considered the leader of the family and the woman is the follower. The woman must take care of all the household chores, cleaning the house and raising the children while the men go outside to find work.

Nowadays, with the rising costs, most women carry the heavy burden of working as well as raising the children. Asian women and Thai women are known as very able and hardworking housewives, which is why foreigners like to marry Thai women, thinking they will get a wife and cleaner at the same time. What a great deal!

The culture that gives importance to the rights and equality of men and women in Finland seems to only work well for European women because they will never ever let their husbands take advantage of them. However, for Thai women who are used to being the follower, they will let their husbands abuse them, using them for hard work, cut them off to the outside world, forbid them from going outside, or even criticize the smell of certain Thai foods.

Lately, when I was invited to be the guest speaker and attend a conference on spousal benefits, such as the rights and duties of the spouse, the management of assets between spouses, the welfare of mother and child, and other important topics, I discovered that most Thai women lacked the knowledge about the law and their rights. Most of this is due to the concealment by their husbands and their lack of interest to find out more knowledge to benefit themselves.

Therefore, I think it is time for Thai women to stand up for their rights. They can start by asking for information from the responsible organizations, of which there are many in Finland, or from the Thai embassy. Most of all, they have to be brave enough to stand up and call for their rights, like European women have done. It is time for Thai women to stop letting themselves be taken advantage of.

Dao's story

I got to know so many stories about Thai women living abroad that I started wanting to compile them into a book to act as a warning to other Thai women. The main burdens for Thai women in Finland are usually their family, husband, and children.

There's the story of one Thai woman that I want to mention in this book to remind other Thai women who want to have a foreign husband that many foreigners are not the angels they dreamed of. Many women met with a horrifying truth when they came to live abroad, like the story of this Thai woman, who I shall call "Dao" here.

Dao told me that before she met her Finn husband, her family came from upcountry and they owned a fruit orchard. She grew up and studied there before attending college in Bangkok. During that time, some talent scouts invited her to attend a beauty pageant and she turned to modeling and fame until she had to drop out of college.

After that, Dao became a public relations staff at a hotel at her friend's suggestion. There, she met a Finn man who introduced himself as an electrical engineer. He usually came to pick her up for dinner, bought her gifts and give her large tips to spend. When he asked her to marry him, Dao thought that it was a great chance to start a new life and to study abroad. The Finn man promised to take care of her and her family well, so she decided to take her to meet her parents to ask her permission to get married in Finland. She prepared to go live abroad with excitement.

Finland was not as beautiful as she dreamed, but when Dao set foot into the apartment of the man she intended to spend the rest of her life with, she nearly went into shock at what she saw. The dreams she had before she reached Finland quickly shattered. She saw an apartment that was as dirty as a rat's nest, and the toilet was so dirty, as if it had not been cleaned for years. The toilet didn't flush.

When she stepped into the house, she had to keep her legs high in order not to kick over the things that were littered in the hallway. The kitchen was in the living room, the sink piled high with unwashed dishes. The apartment was so tiny that it did not have a separate bedroom and they slept on a bed that was in the sitting room. Dao couldn't help but think: she thought that her family was poor, but this apartment was so much dirtier that what she was used to!

Dao tried to collect her thoughts and clean the apartment. She had no other choice but to stay here. The only thing she could do was to set the room as nicely as possible. Her feelings at that time were a world away from when she got on the plane and landed in Finland. When Dao said she was hungry, her boyfriend handed 10 Euros for her to go and buy food, even though she did not know the roads. She had to beg for him to go and buy food for her. Since that day, Dao started to notice that her boyfriend never went to work. He sat at home and drank beer, and sometimes invited friends over to come and drink with him. She had to find food to serve the guests.

One day, Dao couldn't stand her curiosity any longer and asked her boyfriend why he never went to work. His answer stunned her: he told her that he had been unemployed for a year already. She immediately understood that she had been tricked the entire time. Everything that this man promised her was a complete lie.

During that time, she tried to contact other Thai people and the Thai embassy to ask for assistance. She was advised to learn Finnish to increase the chances of finding work. Dao planned to finish her studies, so she asked her boyfriend to keep his promise to marry her. After that, the money that she brought with her from Thailand started to dwindle, but she had to sacrifice part of it to feed the family.

Instead of being grateful, her husband accused her of having an affair and found reasons to hit her. When she could no longer stand it, she asked for a divorce but her alcoholic husband refused, promising to turn over a new leaf and find a job.

The situation should have gotten better when her husband got a job, but the situation got even worse because her husband brought another foreign girl into the house to live with them. Dao felt so cheapened until she no longer felt like a human being. She was like an animal that anyone could abuse however they liked.

That was the reason that I always saw Dao in a disheveled state, with ruffled hair and tattered old clothes. She dared not face her Thai friends and she didn't want to tell her family the truth because she did not want to disappoint them.

Now, Dao is divorced from that disgusting man and she found a stable job. Even though she is only a cleaner, she can see a brighter future now than she saw before. Every time she bends down to clean a toilet bowl, she can still remember the state of the first bathroom she ever saw in Finland. Now, she is making a living out of cleaning toilets, Dao wanted me to tell her story to other Thai women as a reminder for them not to decide to spend their lives with a foreigner that they do not know well enough.

I compared Dao's situation to mine. I also met my husband in a very short time, but fortunately for me, my husband is a true gentleman and his family has been very kind to me. If my husband had shown the opposite character once he got to Finland, my son and I would have been in a difficult position, and I might be no different than Dao today.

Cross-cultural romances do not always end in happily ever after. Giving yourself adequate time to learn about each other's backgrounds will help you avoid false expectations and help Thai women deal with any changes in their married life abroad.

Great and meaningful books

I got to read a great book on the advice of Ajarn Saroj, an elder Thai person in Finland whom I have a lot of respect for. Ajarn Saroj is a knowledgeable and diligent person. He has worked and studied at the same time until he graduated in Finland.

Moreover, he is an frugal person and is careful with money. He has continuously taught me about living life in a mindful way and showed compassion to me as if he was a father of mine.

I felt that meeting someone from your own country who is so compassionate in a foreign land is like getting a magical blessing. I felt like a tree that's been watered fully and ready to blossom. I am so fortunate to have met another good man in the foreign community.

The book that Ajarn Saroj suggested contained some thoughts that helped me to be mindful of living my life. That book is called *"How to Win Friends and Influence People"* by Dale Carnegie. It is highly beneficial and can be applied to modern day experiences and encounters, whether it is in the context of the family or friends at work.

One of the topics which I thought was an important thing that often gets overlooked is *"important lessons for women."* Since the age of time, roses are a universal symbol of love. They are easy to find, especially in the spring time when they are displayed on all the streets. They are cheaper than orchids and easier to find than the Edelweiss that grow on the cliffs of the towering Alps.

Why do husbands need to wait until their wives are lying in hospital to bring her roses? Why don't they find flowers for their wives tomorrow evening? Those who like to experiment should try it and wait to see the results.

These things are facts that I wholeheartedly agree with. They remind us not to let our loved ones lie in hospital before bringing them flowers. We should do it as often as possible. I wish that all husbands were aware of this. I think this world would be more beautiful if all husbands were bringing home flowers for their wives who are busy doing housework. Their tired faces would turn into a big smile when they get the beautiful flowers from their husbands.

Another interesting point was *"There is no such thing as a happy marriage. It is all part of an articulate and cleverly drafted plan."*

I thought that getting a great partner is like winning first prize at the lottery and it is up to fate and luck to decide what happens next, but the book showed me that having the perfect marriage is not up to luck. Spending your life with someone has to follow a cleverly drafted plan, and I found that it is completely true.

This thought reminds us to be considerate and not wait around for luck.

The last thing I want to mention is *"Blindness is the tragedy we all face."* That is, most men would not even think about saying anything to hurt customer in their business, but they would scream and shout at their wives, even though their happiness comes from their married life and not their business.

Most women cannot understand why men can't use their patience to manage the house or organize it in the same way that they organize their business or their profession until it becomes a great success. This is what I agree with most. I am most fortunate that Pasi doesn't say anything or behave in any way that would make me upset.

A lot of my friends have to suffer in their married lives because their husband doesn't speak to them nicely even though they can be very polite when making conversation with strangers. I used to ask my friends why they put up with it and most of them said that they are doing it for the sake of their children because they don't want their children to suffer.

I felt so sorry for them and I wish I could give Dale Carnegie's books to those husbands. People usually overlook the people who are the most precious in their lives and don't realize their true value until they have lost them.

This is the classic mistake that we make as humans. I can only hope that most of them can come to their senses and see sense before it's too late.

My English

Even though I've lived abroad for many years, my English is neither good nor perfect. I never paid much attention to studying and never thought I would be living abroad, since I never thought I would get to use it much in Thailand and I was not interested in the English language. I only started to study English when my family business required me to start communicating with foreigners.

I am a confident person so I can communicate enough to get by, but I have been told that my accent is not good enough so I feel uncomfortable when I speak English. Now on the world stage, whatever form of English you speak, you should be accepted and respected. For example, the Japanese Prime Minister speaks with a strange accent, with Japanese expressiveness, and is a little hard to understand. However he is as well-respected as the British Prime Minister. It is noticeable that every air hostess of every airline speaks English in their national accent. Language is an interesting art to practice.

Linguists nowadays have said that different accents are a beautiful character of the human language as they reflect the art of different pronunciations in different languages. Every person has the same vocal cords but there are different ways to pronounce things. In this world, we give importance to equality and using our accents to judge other people is another form of unforgiveable discrimination.

If sexism and racism is a form of discrimination, discriminating against others for the way they speak must be gotten rid of as well. We should overcome this conservative view and try to catch up with the modern times.

An open view to the world

When I first lived in Finland, I was quite patriotic and I reminded myself to follow Thai traditions even though I was in a foreign land. At the same time I tried to broadcast the uniqueness of being Thai to foreigners, whether it is our delicious food, the beautiful landscape or even with my children, I tried to educate them on the essence of being Thai.

After spending some time in the big world, seeing and learning about art, culture, architecture and history of many other countries in the world, I felt like I had escaped the prisons that enclosed my mind.

When Pasi first took me to other neighbouring countries around Finland, I didn't pay much attention to the architecture or museums there because my mind was focused on the idea that artwork in Thailand is the most intricate and elaborate and unrivaled in the world. As such, my brain was focused on the shopping that was available.

When I went to Russia, the Czech Republic, Italy and many other countries, I felt amazed at many of their historical destinations, their palaces and their castles. All of them are so enormous and beautiful, like a scene out of a dream.

In every place there were invaluable pieces of artwork and paintings by talented national artists. I started to see that every country had a unique beauty and it was hard to judge which country had better art than the other. The old a valuable art and architecture at these places allowed the younger generations to know how about their philosophy, how the people lived, and is a great source of national pride, attracting those who come into the contact with them to study the history of their people.

I'm lucky to be able to travel and experience these great civilizations in many countries, which has helped me to escape my narrow mind frame. I got to know a lot of women who lived abroad who took their families from Thailand to travel to many places in Europe until they changed their opinion of the world. It reminded me of the Chinese proverb, *"Better to travel ten thousands of miles than to read ten thousand books."*

Travel opens our heart to new things and I think it is the good thing about living abroad. You can look forward at the future and look back at your homeland with a different and broader viewpoint.

Compliment or insult?

The exquisiteness of the historical buildings while I was traveling made me gawk and I admired them for having excellent craftsmanship skills. Multiple rooms stretching as far as the eye can see- more than the owners could walk to in a day, left me astounded. They must have spent a fortune hiring so many workers, building such majestic establishments. Those places can tell the visitors so much. The government is clever to let visitors go into those places as a testament to the world of what their people have achieved.

I've been to many countries and looked around their palaces. I don't know if younger generations would feel the same way I did. When I saw them for the first time, I was impressed by their grandeur and I didn't think that I was standing in the present. I thought I was in heaven, like something I had seen in a movie. I didn't think these places existed in real life. .

On the way back I saw some museums that showed how people lived hundreds of years ago: the hardship, the kitchen equipment and people's homes in wartime. The houses acted as a symbol of wealth and class, separating the poor living in poverty and the upper class and the royals.

What bothered me was that rich people have so much money and have more rooms than they can visit in a day, but those who are homeless or have one small home have to live in such cramped conditions. How could their living conditions be so different?

I am not surprised that many countries have changed their system of government to democracy since they want everyone to be equal and have equal rights.

A development

I found out about a professor of Anthropology from the University of Washington who were giving a lecture at Thammasat University Tha Prachan under the topic of *"From farmer to world labour. The modern life of Isaan farmers."* The content spoke of a house survey conducted in Nong Tuen village, Muang, Mahasarakam province 50 years ago.

The surveys were conducted consecutively between 1980-2003 and revealed that 57% of North-East Thailand or Isaan people had high school education or higher and that many Thai Isaan people were working in Bangkok or studied in Bangkok and went back home, taking back their knowledge and experience to make a career, like running a grocery shop, car garage or rice mill, etc., helping to develop their local community. From 1967 onwards, Isaan men and women left to go and work abroad and more got married to foreigners every year.

Those people had the chance to see the outside world and brought back new technology to their homes. Some set up a base abroad where everyone has mobile phones and computers. They can get news access at the same time as everyone else from all corners of the world.

What I wanted to say most is that Thai women who are living abroad have been educated and know foreign languages, and that the language schools abroad do not just teach languages.

These language schools will take the students to learn and go on study trips to various industries, museums, opera, theatre, telecommunications, European countries and computers, etc. In those countries, Thai people gain knowledge and become more modern.

These are things that contribute to a body of knowledge that Thai people living in Thailand do not have a chance to know and study because it is not available in universities. Getting to live abroad is a profit in life as well as getting to travel to neighbouring countries.

That means that villagers can also find news and experiences from abroad, which adds to their education. I think that as human beings, living on the same planet and looking down on each other shows that the problems that we have don't come from people not being educated, but it comes from them having an education that does not teach them to be respectful of other people's humanity. Those people are the uneducated ones.

Chapter 11
My Lifelong Dream

Looking forward and looking back

When I was 15, I heard about disturbing news that filled my head with so many questions. I could not understand the events that took place on 6 October 1976: over 3,000 protesters were killed at Thammasat University, the symbol of thought and ideology.

The army and police, armed with hand grenades, bullets and tear gas descended on the protesters from 5.30 a.m. in the morning until 9 a.m. The brave warriors were brutally beaten and hanged. Some were soaked in fuel and burned alive. Some had stakes put through their chest or through other parts of their bodies. Tens of people died and many were injured. The others were arrested, imprisoned and forced to strip, both male and female, before they were herded into a truck like criminals.

The protestors were framed with doctored pictures of their activities. The photographs were printed in the newspaper. Some papers accused the protestors of lèse majesté and the protestors were brutally rounded up, which was followed by a coup.

After that, there was a widespread sweep to squash the rest of the protestors, charging them with being a threat to society. Some fled to the jungle to live in hiding, as well as having to wrestle with the communist party in the countryside. This is a summary of what happened on 6 October 1976. At that time, I was young and still in school, but what happened could not be erased from my memory. I held on to my curiosity and asked my teacher, but I could not get any clear answers and I was advised to study and only ask the questions that are relevant to my textbooks.

After the events passed, people seemed to forget and no one dared to bring it up for fear of those in power. After that, there were similar events but no one dared to reveal themselves or stand up to the authorities, fearing for their own safety.

In May 2006, there was a military coup to take back power from the democratically elected government, and then in May 2010, demonstrators came out to call on the military government to dissolve the parliament and call for new elections. The dispersal of the protestors was brutal. The soldiers shot 100 people and wounded 2000. The news was broadcast all over the world.

Even in Finland, I got the same news. The pressure I had been carrying inside erupted easily. Wherever I was, I was still a Thai person. Even if I didn't live in Thailand, my family is still in Thailand. I could no longer stand by and do nothing. I tried to check the news and pay more attention, following the international news and putting the brave democracy lovers in my thoughts and prayers.

While I felt sorry for the losses by the families of the fallen ones, I felt that governments formed by coups are always brutal and always try to cover up the truth, like many times before. History was repeating itself. Afterwards, I questioned why those in power would order the killing of unarmed civilians.

Why were nurses in nurses uniforms brutally gunned down? Why did a democratically elected government that came to power by the majority vote get driven out?

Why was the death of innocent people not respected? Why didn't anyone take responsibility for the deaths of the pro-democracy protestors? What was the reason for the coup? What was the reason for killing people and dissolving the parliament? How did people who were not elected become prime ministers?

Why were the news in Thailand different from the news abroad? I had so many other questions. These questions bothered me so much that I had to revise them and study Thai politics again.

The answer was that a small Thai woman like me should not neglect and pretend that I cannot see what is going on. Paying attention to politics and society is not just a job for the men or those living in Thailand. Thais should pay attention, especially hundreds and thousands of us living abroad and our children who have learned about real democracy from Europe. I had to tell myself that and take a look around. The future of Thai children growing up abroad, one day going back to be a major force for the country, taking their model of democracy back to Thailand. It will lead to prosperity and put us on an equal footing with other countries.

At least every Thai abroad has the right to go and vote in their country of residence. From now on, each and every one of their votes will have a true effect on the country. Learning and finding answers from Thailand has allowed us to learn about the past, and voting has an effect on the elected and those casting the vote.

A group of academics previously suggested that voting should be done on a 3 to 1 ratio, meaning 3 uneducated people receive 1 vote and 1 undergraduate receives 1 vote.

I do not know what they use to define uneducated. How do they measure it? Is there an instrument to say this person or that person has no intellect to choose a representative? Some of the thoughts that come out of some of the people who claim to be highly educated are so laughable. Looking down on people who have no education or assuming that Thai women who live abroad should not be accepted, cutting down the rights of other people and overlooking their humanity is clearly racist. It is time for us villagers abroad to take a look and think about the people whom we want to be our representative.

Sightless

It is true that such brutality did not occur in April-May of 2010 but there is another kind of brutality that occurred. The massacre of 6 October 1976 occurred suddenly, forcefully and in cold blood, but ended quickly within 24 hours, since early dawn of the 6th until dusk of the same day. However, the hunting and killing of protesters at Rachadamnoen and Ratchaprasong occurred over a prolonged period of time. There were small clashes in many locations, over and over. Each hour and each day that passed, protestors, journalists and observers were under fire from the soldiers surrounding the protest site, until many injuries and deaths occurred, not to mention being shot at by snipers until many died.

All of these images were published all over the world amidst the cries of joy from some city folk and the inaction of those who claimed that they are pro-peace, against violence, love the people and are fighting for justice.

The cold bloodedness of April- May 2010 occurred because the ruthlessness of the government killings and indifference of city folk who allowed the killings to go on without giving it a second thought. One of the things that I cannot forget to mention are the national poets who achieved their fame from writing for the people, until they are regarded in society as the voice of morality. Where were they at this time, or did they not see the protesters as human beings, therefore their deaths did not mean anything? If that is so, the events of April-May was even more ruthless than 6 October in that not only were the dead denied their humanity, but tens and thousands of protesters in this event get reduced to less than nothing. Were they not fighters for democracy, fighting on behalf of other citizens like in the past? There are many idealists who, over time, may have given up or abandoned the principles that they held dear in the past. Many lawyers who fought to protect the rights of political prisoners in the past have turned into instruments of the regime. Many progressive and educated people dreamed of a flourishing democracy in their youth but as time passed, they became the vocal piece for the coup government. Many writers and poets have abandoned their beliefs in the things they used to write about. They should not call themselves writers and poets anymore because the special status as *"poet"* or *"writer"* that they achieved occurred from their work in the past and from the tireless work of past writers like Khun Kulab Saipradit, who gave being a writer or poet a special status through their sacrifice for the greater good.

Although it is true that the events of April-May 2010 are complex and influenced by many various factors that have been concealed so much that it is difficult to say what is black or white clearly and decisively, refusing to admit the truth that hundreds of people were shot to death and thousands were seriously injured is impossible to understand. In the past, poets like Khun Kulab, Nai Phee, Nai Jit Phumisak, whom these modern poets look up to, have created a memorable example of sacrifice and dedication to fighting for the people. What is stopping these modern poets from seeing what other people can see?

Another possible explanation is that April-May 2010 are different from May 1992 or October 1973 us that the former two ended with the victory of the protestors or at least a change in the leader of the government, so these poets were very comfortable to write in praise of the protestors' sacrifice. Meanwhile, the massacre of April-May 2010 resulted in defeat, much like the massacre of 6 October 1976, which has resulted in the silence of the poets and writers, who have failed to even mention that people died at Ratchadamnoen and Ratchaprasong. If this is the case, the problem of Thai poets and writers may not be because they are in the period of transition of power, as I previously understood. I think Thai society still has many pretenses. It lies and refuses to admit the truth.

People look to the winner to gain their own personal benefits, making them blind to the fact that they are walking into a trap and are helping to indirectly create an injustice. The past declarations of believing in people power and commitment to the fight for freedom and democracy have long been forgotten.

Model Citizens

A Thai magazine invited their readers in their New Year edition to *"gather together to mentally get rid of bad people"*. I started to wonder whether we had the mental capacity to get rid of bad people. The people who think they can telepathically get rid of bad people must believe that they are such good people, or model citizens. What do you use to measure who is good and who is bad? Is there a new computer-like device which measures goodness and badness?... I would really like to buy one so that I can use it on a politician. If we could measure their goodness right then and there, we would get rid of our current problems, of this debate on good or bad. I have a few scenarios for you to compare and consider who is good or bad, for example:

First scenario: I have a law professor who seems like a good, respectable person. He is a good and entertaining lecturer and all the students want to take classes with him because they respect him. One day, he declares that uneducated people or those who live in the provinces should not have as much rights as those living in big cities. He leads his students onto the streets, telling them that it is not necessary to follow the law, allows them to close down government offices, airports, embassies, and calls on the army to stage a coup, disregarding democratic principles. Would you still consider this professor a good person and would you still want to enroll in his classes?

Second scenario: my best friend is a generous person and is kind to everyone around her. She always gives great advice and her family is well-respected and well-liked. One day I found out that they do not treat their servants well at all and act as if they are not human beings. How can I know whether my friend is a good person or a bad person?

Third scenario: a prominent politician is always shown making merit on TV, as well as taking his family to TV shows. On television interviews he says that he loves his family and he takes care of all his kids, sending them to college to get a good education. He declares that he loves his wife on national television until the whole country is so emotionally moved that he is such a family man. One day, the court convicts him of corruption and says that he has mishandled the people's taxes, as well as ordered the mass murder of innocent civilians. Can we really say who is good and who is bad?

At the time of writing, my country is on fire and is on the brink of a civil war. The root cause is a group of people who do not believe in the electoral process and want to have a political system of appointed ministers from their own interest group, claiming that those are good people, model citizens with good ethics, therefore better suited to be prime minister. They claim that people with higher education should have more voting rights than less educated people, and rural voters shouldn't have the same voting rights as urban voters. I don't know what kind of era we are living in. It made me think that I was watching a dramatic soap opera in a scene where the noble family are scolding the rural housemaid, or a scene were the poor heroine was being tormented by a high-society family who despise the rural poor.

In actual fact, my home country is being divided into two. Right now, some families have been split because the family members have different political opinions. The husband supports one cause while the wife supports the other. Each watches different television programs on different TV's and might even turn their backs on each other when they go to bed.

The same story applies to political parties. Siblings from the same family have been known to become members of different political parties. They fight without giving an inch, as if they did not share the same mother. I had the same encounter- a good friend of mine found out that I stood on the side of democracy and equal rights, with one voice getting one vote. She became very unhappy and stopped being friends with me immediately, and even tried to stop me from voting.

The current political situation in Thailand has severe consequences on the daily lives of citizens. I think that having different opinions does not mean that you have to become enemies. In actual fact, it is quite good to have a counterbalance in the democratic system. People that don't agree can demonstrate in peace and debate the issues. However, the end result must respect the majority rule. Even in other countries abroad, the rule of the law is the most important and everybody must live by the same rules in order to live together in harmony.

That is why I am so surprised that there is no respect for the democratic rule in Thailand. There is protesting and harming other people who do not share the same opinion, taking away the liberties of others. The rule of law is not respected. People are encouraged to hate each other and kill each other, until eventually many deaths resulted from the political protest. I am fearful that acting in this way will make the people whose rights have been taken away and people who want democratic elections to also take to the streets to make their voices heard. What will happen then? I can see civil war looming in the distance.

These events have inspired many citizens, university students and groups that support peace to gather together to light candles and tie on white ribbons and white balloons as a symbol for the protestors to stop hurting the country, to put an end to the economic disruption and harm to tourism. Many countries have now cancelled flights to Thailand.

As a Thai person living abroad and closely monitoring the situation, I gathered a group of friends who also support democratic elections and want to use their rights to vote abroad. We congregated outside the White Church in Finland, held placards, lit candles for peace and harmony, protested against a coup d'état and called for elections. This was well-supported by Thai people as well as the media and peace organisations in Finland, who also joined in this symbolic act.

I was overwhelmed and hopeful by the coming together of these people. Nobody wants a civil war to occur because the casualties are the people, who are used as tools for each side as they struggle for power. The losses, injuries and disabilities all happen to Thai people. We all sing the same national anthem, have the same King, and no matter where we go, we tell people that we come from Thailand, why must all the killing occur?

In European country where I live, you can see that there are not that many violent crimes, bodily assaults or violation of the rights of others. That doesn't mean that those countries are inhabited by angels and have a society made up of only good people. However, in order to govern the masses, respecting each other's rights, liberties and rule of law, justice in governmental affairs, education, income and social equality are the key. When people do not come out to hurt each other, it doesn't mean that they are good people, but it means that they respect the rule of law and each other's rights. In the same way, when politicians and bureaucrats are not corrupt, it doesn't mean that they are angelic politicians who only do good. Rather, it means they are scared of the punishment by law and societal pressure, which stops them from being corrupt.

Who to choose? What is the way out?

With the help of the Internet, people can learn from technology and find information in many ways, for instance The Economist and The New York Times write about Thai politics. YouTube, Democracy School, DNN News Thailand, the Thai Post newspaper, cable TV, Voice TV, Kid Hen Len Tang program, Asia update,

Diva's Café and many other sources of information on the Internet allow Thai women living abroad to get uncensored information. Therefore, Thai people living abroad have the full information to know who to choose or who not to choose.

These things are important for people living abroad because we still have family in Thailand who could be affected by a bad government. Having a voting booth in the embassy is a beneficial and most valuable thing.

All Thai people can use their voting rights with pride. How do we know who to choose? Teaching and giving truthful knowledge about Thai history is important.

Parents should tell the truth to the children and members of the family so that everyone in the family can see the light. They can find the news or evidence on the Internet. Letting Thai people abroad know the difference is helping to open their eyes and letting them see the light. You are helping the country indirectly.

Conflict causes change

I want to see a change happen in Thailand, such as strong politics which respects human rights. Any change usually arises from conflict and fighting, but not the kind of fight where guns are pointed at each other.

That is, making a political stand and debating with the side that doesn't agree. The conflict will only end when you respect the majority and will be resolved by going back to elections, with elected representatives acting as the voice of the people.

Anyone who wants to be a representative can run for office. It's that simple. No one should have the right to claim to seek change and then set up an unelected government. These people are despicable and scary. Thai people should not give power to them. How can you know that they know better than everyone else? There is no thermometer for goodness. Elections, on the other hand, can be measured.

Holding elections under the democratic process do not mean that you will get the best person to govern, but you will get someone who deals with the people under an agreed set of rules, the same rules as everyone else.

The stakeholders in society have to bargain, including the farmers, workers, major businesses, small businesses, salarymen and government officials.

All of these groups have their own interests to protect and they will use these processes to bargain for power. All of these processes can be done in parliament. If the negotiations cannot be achieved in the lower house, there is still a chance to fight it out on the streets under the agenda of the stakeholders. I think it is clearer and simpler if the debate is done under rules, but if you choose people who are corrupt and don't follow the agreement, there has to be a mechanism in the democratic process to question them and call for the dissolution of parliament. The representatives should resign and new elections should be called forth.

None of these should be handled by a coup d'etat, which strips away all the rights of the media and the liberties of the citizens. It is closing the door on the political experiences of the people. I am a foreign woman living abroad and many Thai women still want democracy. When our democracy strengthens and the minority accepts the majority, Thailand will finally be a true democracy like many other countries in the world.

An Event for the story book

I cannot believe that I would live to see such events, which should go down in the history books. Even though I had finished writing this book and it was on its way to print, I had to recall it back to write once more. At the time of my writing, there are events which I have to get into writing to tell our future generations this important part of history.

There are events taking place in Thailand which have grabbed the attention of the world. That is, the protest of a minority of the population who do not want elections and have tried to stop others from accessing the poll booths on pre-election day. The footage that has appeared before the world is that those who love democracy and want to use their vote having to pass through barricades of protesters. Some have even been seriously injured. Most of all, a woman had to beg for the door to the polling station, which had been chained up, to be opened.

When the protesters would not cooperate and savagely tried to get in the way, she woman climbed the gate to get inside to vote. When she got to the other side, the election official applauded her, helped her to a polling booth and said, *"You were very brave"*. That woman was the first person to cast the vote at that polling station that day.

The events that happened, as well as the bravery of those who wanted to cast their vote on election day, must be remembered by the world. It has caused millions of Thai people to wake up and protect their freedom and their rights and given them the courage to express themselves.

I am amazed and I want to loudly applaud her. I think that differences of opinion can happen anywhere. What is most important is how we can coexist without being enemies. The only thing that can make people live together in harmony is the respect for the law and the rights of others. These are the rules which are respected the world over which everyone has used as a guideline to live peacefully together.

Thai politics in the eyes of foreigners

Thanks to technology, I know how the world looks at Thai politics. On 9th December, between 9.30 p.m. - 10.00 p.m., a world news channel of Feng Huang TV station in Hong Kong reported an analysis by one of their famous analysts, who is respected by millions of Chinese people.

The analyst described the chaos in Thailand as being caused by the new Constitution of 2007, which is the new constitution drafted after the coup that overthrew the government of Thaksin Shinawatra. It is one of the most ridiculous and senseless constitutions, and the longest and most detailed one in the world.

There is no other constitution in the world that includes so much detail. The 2007 Constitution of Thailand is over 300 pages long. It is so detailed that any action or any utterances of every citizen is speculated in the constitution. Whatever you do, there is a high chance that you will violate the constitution. For example, the ex-prime minister Samak Sundaravej was indicted with violation of the constitution and had to be removed from his position because he was on television teaching a cooking show.

As I'm writing this, the constitutional court has admitted their mistake on the ruling of the Samak Sundaravej case regarding the cooking show and the dissolution of his political party, admitting they made their decision too hastily. I felt sorry for his poor soul, who did not live to see the day of his judgment. As well as this, the way the political party was dissolved was too simple. In a political party, if 1 or 2 of the executives make a mistake or commit a small wrongful act, that party would be dissolved and people who are not guilty would be disqualified as well.

Therefore, this constitution should be amended. But the allies that are against the government are against the change in the constitution. Even their opinion goes against democracy. They think that western democracy, or the one man one vote system, should not apply to Thailand. They think that farmers in the villages are not capable of using their right to vote in the one man one vote system.

They proposed a new political system with 50% of the representatives of the house coming from elections and 50% coming from appointment. What is worse is that some of the protestors from the allies took over Government House for more than two months, which is a senseless act. After that, they took over parliament, which means that democracy was completely violated. I only looked at some of the articles to understand. I think that Thailand is in a situation where foreigners are very interested about the chaos that is going on. I don't know when it is going to end. There is no convenient solution because there are people that don't agree and would do anything to stop it. I closely monitor the news and pray that there is a bloodless solution. I want to see my relatives in Thailand and those of us living abroad get the chance to exercise our rights to speak our thoughts and express our opinions, even if they are different.

The following is a transcript of the section on Thailand in Lee Kuan Yew

The arrival of Thaksin Shinawatra permanently changed Thai politics. Before he came onto the scene, the Bangkok establishment dominated all sides of the political competition and governed largely to the benefit of the nation's capital. If there had been disagreements among the Bangkok elite, none were quite as ferocious as the ones to come. Nor were any of the quarrels as divisive as those that arose during and after Thaksin's term. What Thaksin did was to upset the apple cart of the Thai political status quo by diverting to the poorer parts of the country resources that had previously been hogged by Bangkok and its middle and upper-class residents. Thaksin's was a more inclusive brand of politics that allowed the peasants from the north and the northeast to share in the country's economic growth. A gulf had already existed before his arrival, created by the Bangkok-centric policies of his predecessors. All he did was to awaken the people to the gulf - and the unfairness of it - and to offer policy solutions to bridge it. If he had not done so, I am convinced that somebody else would have come along to do the same.

When he took over the premiership in 2001, Thaksin was already a successful businessman and a billionaire. But if rich Thais were counting on him to show class solidarity, they would soon be sorely disappointed. He implemented policies that favoured the rural poor to an unprecedented extent. He extended loans to farmers, overseas scholarships to students from rural families and government - subsidised housing to the urban poor, many of whom had migrated to the cities in search of jobs and could only afford to live in slums. His healthcare plan targeted at those who could not pay for their own medical insurance provided coverage at just 30 baht (about US$1) per hospital visit.

To Thaksin's opponents, he was turning the country upside down. They were not about to let him get away with it. They called him a populist and claimed his policies would bankrupt the state. (Remarkably, this did not stop them from continuing many of these policies and coming up with other similar ones when they held power from December 2008 to August 2011.) They accused him of corruption and favouring his family businesses, charges he denied. They were also unhappy with his firm - some say dictatorial - handling of the media and his controversial war on drugs in the south of the country, during which due process and human rights may sometimes have been overlooked. Nevertheless, the peasants, overwhelming in numbers, ignored the criticisms and re-elected him in 2005. The Bangkok elite ultimately could not tolerate the man. He was overthrown in a military coup in 2006.

Thailand's capital has since experienced great upheaval. Scenes of chaos have broken out repeatedly on the streets of Bangkok since 2008, with mass protests involving either the Yellow Shirts, who oppose Thaksin and do so in the name of defending the monarchy, or the Red Shirts, made up of Thaksin's ardent supporters. But the latest general election, held in 2011, which handed Thaksin's sister Yingluck the premiership, was a clear vindication by the Thai electorate of the new path that Thaksin had chosen for Thailand. The peasants of the north and the northeast of the country, having tasted what it was like to have access to capital, were not going to give that up. Thaksin and his allies have now won five general elections in a row, in 2001, 2005, 2006, 2007 and 2011. For

Thaksin's opponents to try to hold back the tide is futile.

Despite the recent ferment in Thai society, there is cause for optimism in the long run. The Red Shirts will continue to outnumber the Yellow Shirts for a long time because the latter group draws from a shrinking constituency. The younger generation already holds a less reverent view of the royal family. Furthermore, even though King Bhumibol Adulyadej is a well-respected figure, much of the prestige and magic associated with him will go when he passes on.

The army has always played a central role in Thai politics. It has made sure that no movement against the monarchy, from which it derives its strength, is allowed to raise its head. It too, however, will have no choice but to accept and to adapt to the changed situation. It is after all untenable to resist the will of the electorate for a protracted period. Given time, its ranks will also be filled by soldiers from a younger generation, less enamoured with the monarchy. The military leaders will continue to insist on privileges and will not be content with being reduced to an ordinary army. But they will also learn to live with a government made up of Thaksin's allies. It may even be possible for the army to accept

Thaksin's eventual return to Thailand, if he can promise to get along with them and not pursue any vendettas.

There can be no reverting to Thailand's old politics, to the pre-Thaksin era when the Bangkok elite had a monopoly on power. Thailand will continue moving along the path that Thaksin first steered the country onto. The gap in living standards across the country will narrow. Many peasants will be lifted into the middle class and will help drive the country's domestic consumption. Thailand will do well.

The caste system abroad

My days in Finland encouraged me to know that there is no class or caste system in Finland or Europe. I have never seen it.

The Finnish tax system has included land reform, inheritance tax and very strict land tax. The revenue that you get cannot be kept secret, the comings and goings must be explained and all taxes must be paid according to the law, without any loopholes. If there is any indication that there has been tax evasion, the offender will get fined in arrears or risk going to jail.

All of the citizens of Finland are aware of this law, therefore there is no class system and no taking advantage of each other. People in Europe are very equal to each other and respect each other's right. Most importantly, they are very democratically-minded. Even though they may not be satisfied with the majority voice, everyone respects the rule of law and patiently waits for the next election to express their political opinion again. Therefore, politics in Finland is strong and there are no bloodbaths like some countries or even my home country, for instance.

Amazing Thailand

It sounds so good and it sounds like Thailand must be richer than Japan, America and so many other countries in the world.

Thailand has so many natural resources and most importantly Thailand is an attraction that pulls in foreign interests by itself. Many people visit Thailand, spending hundreds of thousands each time. In each year, billions of baht flows into the country. Where does the money go? It doesn't go into the pockets of the people but ends up in monopolistic businesses that have had a monopoly over the industries for as long as we can remember. Whatever revenues may increase, Thailand is still poor and Thai people are still poor.

Actually, Thailand is rich with natural resources and we are amongst the largest exporters in the world. However, farmers and labourers are still the poorest of all and continue to be in a vicious cycle of poverty. This has given rise to foreign labourers migrating abroad. I'm not surprised why the middlemen and owners of businesses get richer and richer, move all their money abroad, and Thailand becomes poorer and poorer until all our neighbours have overtaken us. This is why Yingluck Shinawatra has had to work so hard to revive the economy. It is an uphill task, but the Thai people are behind her. I am also rooting for her with every breath.

Stepping past your fears

After the repeated coups, everyone is beginning to wake up and ask what the other countries that have been through this have done. It depends on that country whether they want to find out the truth and want to hand back justice to those who have been affected and compensate them for their losses. Two countries that have done that have overcome violent situations well are Germany and Japan. Germany in particular has done very well by apologizing to the Jewish people, whereas in Japan's case it may have been more difficult, but they have also apologized.

As for Thailand, the structure of the politics has never changed, so change is difficult. Those who are involved in the past events are still in power and are resistant to the truth being exposed.

Comparing to Germany and Japan, they have both moved past this and they are fully flourishing democracies. The leaders of those days have all disappeared, making way for new generation leaders who understand the country's history and understand growth. For Thailand, it is like a revolving door where you enter and get stuck and cannot get out. One part of the population also doesn't want to know anything, talk about anything and don't want to mention the past.

They don't want to compare Thailand to any other country. They think that Thailand is the best, the greatest, and don't want to look at the outside world. Also, the people that were involved in those days' events and do not want the events to be investigated are the soldiers and the army. Even now, they have a large part in today's politics. Therefore, this revolving door is inescapable.

The situation has not changed because some of the groups have not changed. They are scared that if things did change, it might affect their way of life. In actuality, it may change it for the better. However, those interest groups cannot risk it. If they had the foresight to do so, it might lead to social and political development, but this has not happened yet in Thailand. Everything is about make-believe and there is no advancement in the education system. The education system must be revamped so that children understand our real history. The truth might be painful to learn today, there may be some people who have to be punished, but all of this is necessary for moving forward. Like the Khmer Rouge, who took a long time before accepting everything that happened, but recently, the leaders have successfully been put to trial before the Cambodian and the world court.

There is no reason that Thailand can't do the same. 36 years has brought some hope that it could. Nowadays, it is still fortunate that the foreign media can report the truth even though everyone in Thailand has been blinded. Last May in 2010, CNN and BBC reported the news of the killing of civilians and provided enough evidence to make Thai people wake up. It is a shame that people in Thailand didn't get this information but everyone else all over the world did. In 2013, the whole world is watching to see whether the person who ordered the killing of 100 civilians and wounded 2,000 others will be brought to justice. The Thai court has been following up on the case. The people who were affected during the military crackdown have stepped forward until the killer has spent all his time going to court without much time to do anything else. Now, Thailand will finally get to see justice.

Questionable work
from the appointed government after the coup

I had a chance to watch a program by the Thai Health Promotion Foundation; it was a drawing competition and the winner was a picture of an alcoholic who gradually turned into a dog.

The pictures made me confused and raised a lot of questions. The meaning of the picture threatens human rights completely, putting people who drink on the same level as animals or thinking of them as lowly as a dog. It is as if they do not think Thai people have the presence of mind to make their own decisions.

I felt sorry that the budget that comes from taxes from the sales of alcohol and tobacco, which totals 24 billion baht over 10 years, has gone towards this kind of marketing and advertising instead of encouraging Thai citizens to have a healthy lifestyle.

In my opinion, everything comes down to the question whether the Thai Health Promotion Foundation had taken a portion of that budget to examine and control the producers of alcohol and question them about their raw materials, or checked on the beansprouts in the markets to see whether they are bleached or have been dipped in formaldehyde, or whether the vegetables in the markets have been processed with chemicals. That is the real and dangerous threat to people's lives and it has been grossly overlooked by the Foundation.

Prohibiting the sales of alcohol between 10 a.m. and 6 p.m. is totally ridiculous. I don't think it helps anything at all, rather than to strip down personal choices, which the government doesn't have the right to do. The Thai Health Promotion Foundation doesn't have the right to say that people can't drink or buy alcohol as gifts. It is stripping down our democratic rights indirectly. I've been living in Finland for 13 years and have seen so many drunk people that it is considered normal.

In Europe, people have the right to drink and get drunk. If anyone chooses to drink until they die, it is up to them to know whether to choose to live or die. People's lives are their own and they have to make their own choices. The government doesn't have the right to interfere with this or force them to do something else.

I have never seen anyone drink themselves to death in Finland. On the contrary, the government even protects drunken people. If anyone is drunk on the side of the road or in a public space, the police will help them get to safety or drop them off at home, which is something I see very often in Finland.

Sometimes I see a policeman carrying a drunkard who refuses to cooperate. It is a funny sight which is regarded as no big deal. Plus, I have never seen advertising on TV that prohibits drinking. There are no signs telling people what they can and can't do. Everyone lives normally. Therefore, the fact that they are using the budget to promote something that takes away our basic human rights demonstrates that the government is interfering with human rights and people are following along without protesting or questioning. The Thai Health Promotion Foundation interferes with people's bodies without thinking anything of it, and will probably continue to do so.

The light at the end of the tunnel

I used to ask myself how my country is going to survive, and how we are going to do it. How can we live in the present situation? I was sure that after the 2006 coup, Thailand would not be the same as before and whatever happened,

Thailand would never return the situation to the old days before the coup. I was delighted with the events that happened which had never been seen before in history, all the intellect and bravery that unprecedentedly took place. Magazines were being produced which I never thought I would get a chance to read, written by those with strong ideologies and great bravery: Fah Deow Gan magazine, Phrai Nee Ka magazine and Matichon, to name a few.

I was excited and happy to see journalists, writers, academics and young new thinkers try to find a way forward for the society with maturity, based on the principles of democracy.

The catalyst for change is the power of the people who stood up to demand their rights and build a strong wall which has been on a strong base of past events. This iron wall will act as a strong shield for the government that has been elected by the people and prevent from executing any more coups. I stand in line with these iron walls, a movement happening in and outside Thailand. The country has to keep moving forward with democracy and faith at its core.

What the people have seen and experienced is only the beginning, but it is the truth. I dreamed about going back home and being close to my mother who is getting older and waiting for the day when her family would return home. Admittedly, the distance between us scares me.

I dreamed about having coffee with my friends and reminiscing about the past. I have thought of ways to do business and bring money back to my home country, as well as taking my beloved husband back of course. I dreamed about the society that is full of smiles and prosperity. My time abroad is probably coming to an end very soon since Finland is not my motherland, not where I grew up. I am waiting to return to Thailand.

Chapter 12
Whose World Is It?

A world without safety

I got the chance to see the ceremony commemorating 1 year of the Oslo bombings and the Utoya Norway shootings, which took many victims from the Worker's Youth League on 22 July 2011.

The losses of that day is undoubtedly one of the worst since World War II, only second to the bombings of the passenger train in Madrid, Spain in 2004. The massacre at Utoya took 68 unfortunate victims and wounded many others. The youngest victim was only 14 years old, and amongst one of them was a Thai woman. For Norwegians and Europeans, this is an unforgettable tragedy.

The most shocking thing is that the perpetrator is only one man with a right wing extremist tendency. He claimed to be in the right wing extremist group and said that what had happened was cruel but necessary. He had to take action against the government's policy which was turning Norway into a multi-racial society, as well as wanting to express his hatred against Muslims.

The confession of this crazy killer made me think about my mother's warning before I came to live in Finland. My mother warned me, *"Do you think you're making the right decision? Will they let you live in a country that's not your own? How are you going to live? Plus, living in other people's country is not going to be as safe as living in your own country."* At that time, I understood that my mother didn't want my son and me to live in a place that she was not sure about. Afterwards, once I had moved to Finland, I would reassure my mother that Scandinavia is one of the most democratic and safe countries in the world.

I thought that racism and religious killings would not happen in these countries, but it seems like I was wrong. It seems that day by day, the massacre of innocent civilians is spreading to every corner of the world. Even in Finland, which is considered the most peaceful country in the world, snipers have shot at people, killing and injuring them. My friend who works not far from that area said that she narrowly escaped death, since she walked past that area not long before the shooting incident occurred.

Nowadays, it seems there is no safe place in the world. As long as we hold on to our prejudices and believe that our own race, religion or beliefs is the most supreme, as long as we hate other human beings with different beliefs, the killings will never end.

Even Thailand, which is considered a country where Buddhists and Muslims live together in peace is still suffering from terrorist bombings and sniper shootings on a daily basis. The question is, how do we live in a world where safety cannot be guaranteed? What do we teach our children when they need to face these threats?

I admire the response of the Norwegian government and the Norwegian people in handling this tragedy. They chose to display love and unity in this situation instead of expressing anger and hatred in the 1 year anniversary of this event. Hundreds and thousands of Norwegians carried roses as they walked along the street and sang along for the families of the victims. The scene looked like a giant blanket of flowers moving forward to say *"Love over hate."*

At the same time, the Norwegian government has come forward to claim that they will stick to democratic principles, respecting liberty and humanity, and they will not respond with force, but instead will use the justice system to determine what is right and wrong.

Even with a suspect is accused of a heinous crime, they are afforded their basic rights during deliberation and are treated as if they are a normal suspect in a crime. This shows that Norway will not give in to hate and will not abandon the principle of humanity.

I think that the actions of the Norwegian people correspond with the Buddhist teachings of forgiveness and good winning over evil. If we face hate and prejudice from other people who share this planet with us, the best thing we can do is to use tolerance and focus our energy on doing positive things instead of letting hatred and retaliation take over. A high-level executive in Norway said, *"The only way we can beat terrorism is to show how much we are better than them. The aim of the terrorists is to lure us into the game of shadows and we should not let them win. That is, we should use the good in us as the guiding light. Then, the world will never be in darkness."*

Even though Finland has laws that ensures equality and protects citizens against discrimination or preferential treatment, they are just laws. Foreigners living abroad cannot do anything but be careful and behave according to the rules and the law. However, you can never know which groups do not agree about the presence of foreigners or which groups discriminates against others. They do not want other nations to become a part of their country and this has given rise to the nationalists or right wing extremists.

The example set by Norway gave a foreigner like me the chills and I prayed that Finland would have some laws to protect foreigners and be open to humanity, sticking to democratic principles as much as Norway. However, the cruelty and brutality displayed by those events have been unforgettable for a foreigner living abroad like me.

I used to dream that one day I will go back to Thailand, to the country where I grew up. Even still, I am not sure where would be a safe place, as long as there is hatred all over the world. However, I am willing to spend my last days in my homeland amongst the warmth of my loving family.

Black or white, we are all human

As I watched the London Olympics 2012's opening ceremony waiting to see the Thai athletes, I had to wait a long time since there were many countries all over the world in attendance.

I was excited to see the faces of people from countries I had never seen before, and the joy of all the athletes who were in awe to be part of the competition. There were hundreds of languages, cultures, religions and everyone was determined to compete in a world that believes in peace and harmony.

When the competition started, in all the games I saw joking, patting, and laughter. Those people probably never knew each other from before and never met before. They all had their own corner of the world and their own religion, but the picture that meets your eyes has impressed the world beyond belief.

Living together and competing in the games has helped to build harmony. Some have even stayed in touch after the games ended. I applaud the Olympics, which has made the world see that there are people in the world that we have never seen or heard of. If I had not watched the Olympics, I would have never known that there are different people from all races and different appearances.

They are all humans in the world just like us and no country is better than the other. There are examples of countries that think they are bigger and more developed but lost in the sports to other smaller countries that other people never knew existed before.

No matter what your skin colour is, everyone has their own abilities, which is no less than others. Competing in sports has let the world know about fellow friends from other races and from other countries. It helps to lessen the hatred and prejudice towards other races and religions. Those people who think that their nation or their religion is superior to others and is the best in the world are probably dying of hatred and rage.

I pray that one day, those people will open their eyes to see and accept the truth. When that day comes, the world can finally live in peace and harmony. I really hope so.

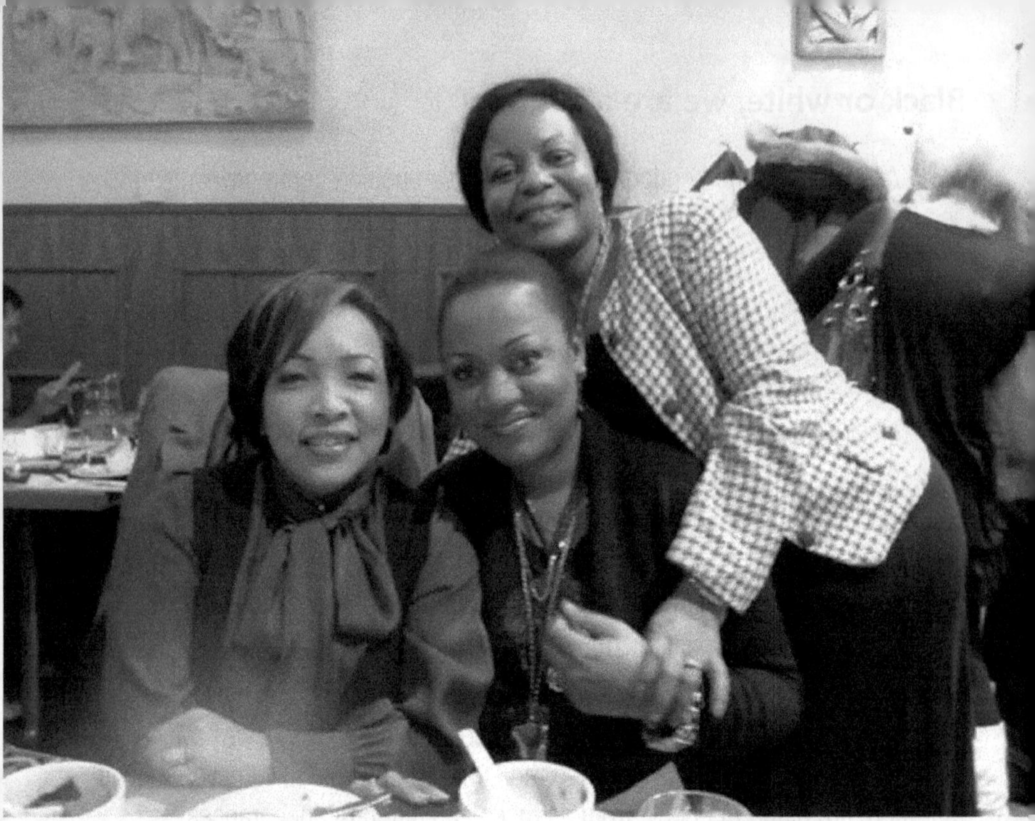

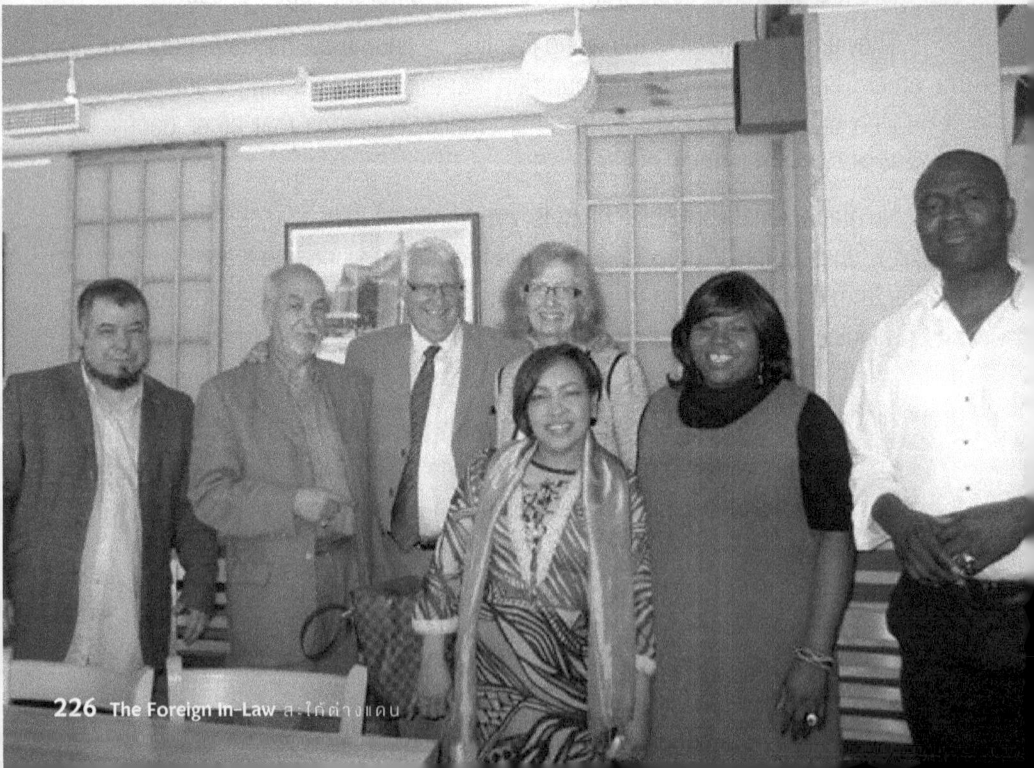

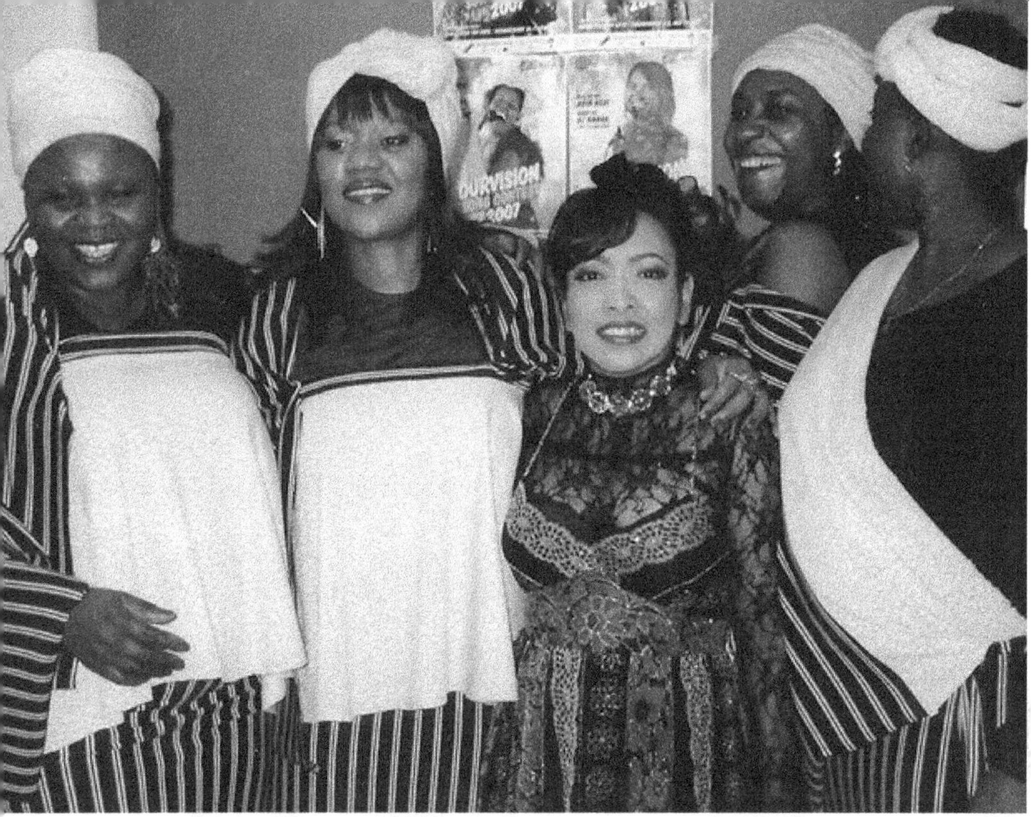

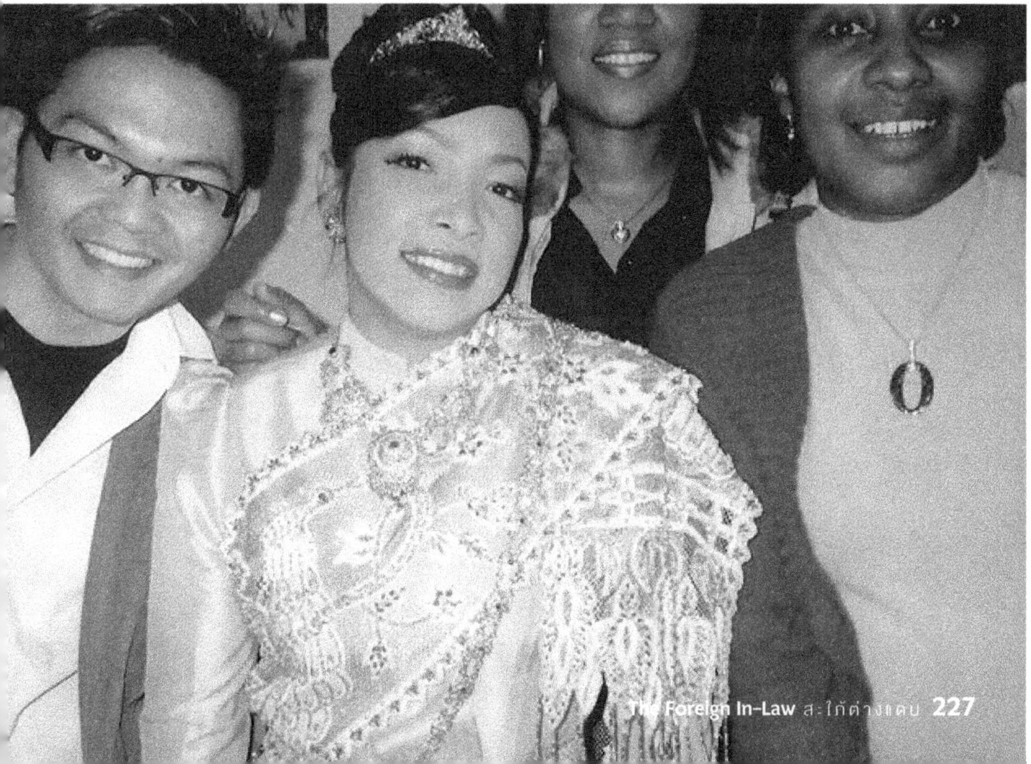

Acknowledgements

I hope that **The Foreign In-Law** will be somewhat useful to the reader. My intention was to tell the story of a life of a Thai woman living in a foreign country, and to give the opinions and perspectives I gained from my experiences, past to present.

All of the stories in this book are my pride and joy, and I am privileged to be able to tell many of them to you, even though some of them may be outspoken or different from what the reader might think. However, I want the reader to be free to think, and to be free to think differently. Some of the stories I tell may make you think and chatter amongst yourself, and in that way you add value to my story. Looking back at all the changes, we may have forgotten how time has changed us or what our experiences have taught us, which makes the stories much more precious.

Most of all, I hope that this book will help Thai people living abroad to recount our history and learn that there are many things in this world we do not know. I hope that we can become part of the effort to make our motherland more prosperous, more developed, and more democratic so that we can become equal to many other countries in the world. I hope that the reader can find themselves and discover their passion, their talents, and spark a change within themselves, whether by thinking or doing. Today is not too late, and I hope I can be your inspiration and encouragement in your efforts to do so.

I would like to thank all of my readers for supporting this book. I am delighted to share some of my stories with you, in case you should ever come across the same experiences one day.

I hope I can provide some inspiration, and I pray that all of you will have a happy family and a happy life.

Porntipa Ilvesmäki

About the author

I met Tiki for the first time around June 2000. It was the summer and the first thing we noticed was that she was beautiful and petite. When we spent some time with her, it was clear to see that she is very helpful and a hardworking woman.

I experienced all of these things for myself, for example, after the meal, she would start washing the dishes straight away even though she was pregnant at the time and her mobility was much lessened. Her hard work was plain to see and became more evident as the days go on.

The more I know her, the more I know what a diligent person she is. A wife like Tiki is so good for my son that there can be no other replacement. We met at Kajaani and I remember her comparing me to her father, Khun Prateung.

The next day, we drove from Kajaani to Hyrynsalmi, to the family vacation home. Tiki loved the quiet and the atmosphere there. After that, she liked to go there every time the family came to visit. Our daughter-in-law is the world's most wonderful cook. We have seen her talents many times when she would cook for the family. The whole family would happily sit down to a delicious meal. Tiki is also a talented seamstress. She made a beautiful dress for my wife Inkeri and even mended some of our old clothes. She is also a wonderful singer.

She is also good at other handicrafts, for instance flowers made from fish scales, fruit carving and soap carving to make little flowers, which look truly incredible. The more I know her, the more I see how hardworking, helpful and talented she is. She respects me and at the same time, I respect her. At the same time, a daughter-in-law like Tiki is truly a godsend for my family.

Ilkka Ilvesmäki
(Pasi's Father)

About the author

The first time I met Tiki was in Singapore. I was working or a Tele-operation start up and every Thursday evening I would go out on the town. At that time, Tiki had just broken up with her boyfriend. She was beautiful. I fell in love with her at first sight.

She was an open person and told me many stories without any reservations. After a few days, we saw each other again, and I invited her to my apartment. At that time we were able to talk and exchange all kinds of stories. I was captivated with her storytelling because it seemed so natural, and each and every story made me more and more interested in her.

After that day, I invited her for dinner and a stroll around Singapore. She seemed to be happier than when I first met her and later, I asked her to move from her hotel and stay with me, using the excuse that hotel fees are very expensive. Since then, she has lived with me.

After that, I got to eat delicious meals every day. All of my clothes were washed and ironed neatly. She was beautiful, kind-hearted and was very skilled in cooking and running the household.

Most importantly, when I was with her, she would talk about entertaining things an put a smile on my face the entire time. When I was sure about our future, I asked her to come to Finland with me, and she was brave enough to accept.

She told me that wherever I went, no matter how hot or cold, she would gladly follow me everywhere because she loved me. We got engaged and she made a ring in the shape of the letter P with my surname, Ilvesmäki, engraved on it and surrounded by 21 diamonds. P was the initial of her name, Porntipa, for me.

We travelled back from Singapore to Thailand to ask for her family's permission to bring her son, Kittipong, who was 9 years old, to come to live in Finland together.

It was not easy. Her mother did not seem to agree and didn't want her to come to Finland because of the distance. She was worried about her youngest daughter and her grandson, whom she cared about deeply, but nothing could stop Tiki.

She insisted on coming to live with me until her mother and her family had to give in. After that, Tiki and I lived in Finland together. I was glad and very happy to have her and her son with me, and I fully intended to take care and protect her forever, as I had promised her.

After she came to Finland, we had two more children. I was overjoyed and Tiki did not let me down. She made me proud and my family loves and respects her very much.

Tiki is a capable woman and I never thought that a Thai woman like her would have so many talents. She would constantly surprise me with new talents, and at the same time, she is very giving and always willing to help others.

I am so proud of the fact that she has a good heart and always thinks of helping others.

I am very lucky to have met Tiki, a petite Thai woman. Even if our goals change in the future, we can be together forever.

Lastly, I would like to thank Tiki's family for allowing her to come and live with me. I promise to love and take care of her till death us apart.

Pasi Ilvesmäki

About the author

I remember the first time we met very vividly. It was in Singapore, February 2000. I had been there a few days as a visitor and had fallen in love with the city state, where everything was unbelievably clean and tidy, the vegetation was tropical and luxurious and the people were polite. Everywhere you looked, there were diligent employees swiping streets or trimming bushes. Everyone seemed to have a task, and people passing by were greeted happily. Was this even true? Or was I wearing rose-tinted glasses? I was also flabbergasted by the overwhelming number of book stores, the incomprehensible selection of oriental goods in the markets, and public toilets that were self-cleaning. There were big video screens on the walls of department stores as well as 3-D movies and laser shows that Finland didn't have yet at that time.

I was on my daily walk looking for new attractions when an unknown beauty and Pasi from Finland, whom I knew very well, walked hand-in-hand and appeared from the crowd. This meeting felt as unreal as everything else I had seen in there. Pasi's new companion seemed very delightful, exotic, Asian, yet modern like a Westerner. She was very friendly: it was you, for the first time! I was as enthusiastic about our short meeting as everything else I had experienced in Singapore.

Immediately after seeing you I realized that Pasi, a friend and a long-time partner of my sister was lost in a field of attraction, even if he was not a *"butterfly"* but a kind and responsible IT immigrant from Finland.

Our sudden meeting on the busy Singapore's Orchard Road 'catwalk' high street felt in some odd fashion premeditated and natural, even though it was a complete coincidence. Pasi had been the partner of my sister for seven years, and although their relationship had been stormy for several years, I could not believe that they had truly separated.

Porntipa, you were the reason for me getting tickets to Singapore to spend the winter holiday there with my sister. A gentleman couldn't announce these kinds of news by a text message from the other side of the globe. It was a nice thought but unfortunately, the great holiday did end painfully.

The starting point for a new friendship in Finland, as well as the continuing of an old friendship, was not off to a good start due to this problematic and highly emotional background. It speaks of your courage, and probably Pasi's as well, that you weren't afraid of my opinion and wanted to meet me and my family anyway when moving north.

From the very first meeting at my house you suggested that we could make a meal together. In the beginning I thought it was a bit odd, but I agreed anyway because it meant that I didn't need to think about what to offer for dinner. I had heard about your cooking skills from Pasi several times and I was not a master chef.

A happy looking couple arrived for the first visit accompanied by a rice cooker and all the necessary ingredients. I got to work as your helper with the cooking. A potentially awkward visit instantly felt like a natural beginning. Our discussion was very down-to-earth and broken English covered all the communication that was needed. Our getting acquainted happened naturally while cooking.

In the end, the seemingly odd idea proved to be a very clever thought indeed. You created a versatile meal with my assistance and we could invite the others to eat. They were already hungry and enticed by the gorgeous smell of the spices. The meal was of course heavenly and delicious, and it was easy for us all to continue our discussions by praising the new, incredible tastes and asking again and again the odd names of the spices that went into each dish.

Both my husband Ahti and our two daughters Viivi and Iina (at that time 11 and 8 years) were sincerely thankful for the food. Pasi was looking as happy as ever. As the saying goes, the way to a man's heart is through his stomach and the same applies for women and children.

After the tasty meal you started to tell us your story. You talked about the difficult years of your childhood, and about your family, especially of your mother who taught you to cook, as well as things of your sister and brother. You told about your previous jobs and how you met Pasi. You had the keys of friendship in your possession, and you were willing to use them. You, Porntipa, became Tiki to us.

Your communication with Pasi on the early days of your relationship seemed a bit peculiar to us as an old couple. Because the common language was not quite present, Pasi often used gestures to 'command' you. These simple gestures had become familiar to me in Singapore when ordering a taxi, snapping fingers and pointing 'here'. Practical, I guess, but maybe not so polite in a relationship? You didn't seem too bothered by this, but rather laughed at Pasi. And these gestures haven't been seen for ages.

In the past twelve years we have met in various parties and during our spare time. Your Buddhist wedding ceremony was a particularly beautiful and touching memory. When Jussi was born, we visited him in Kätilöopisto, and when we were invited to be godparents to Jasmin, it was a great sign of trust, and made us even closer.

We have celebrated baptisms, confirmations, and school graduation of our children as well as birthdays together. We have been in various concerts and opera, and spent so many New Years Eve's together. You have flooded my family with splendid handmade gifts. Your skilled hands form flowers not only from traditional vegetables but also from colored stockings, fish scales or soap... It's a miracle to see carrots, beetroots, cucumbers, melons and whatever concretely flourish from your carving. You have always offered your help with catering and decoration for parties. Once when visiting Thailand you had fabulous handmade evening dresses made for Viivi and Iina. You have also taught our girls how to wear makeup as I'm more "natural" and not very familiar with this.

Highlights include also the numerous meals you have offered in your home or in the different restaurants where you have worked. We here in the North can only wonder. The deliciousness of the Thai kitchen is so far from our pragmatic tradition. I guess it's the scarcity of our nature that has molded us and our kitchen. Our flavors are created from simplicity, like for example new potatoes with butter and herring, or New Year's potato salad, and sausages. They are mild in comparison to your Thai meals. I'll have to admit that in the beginning I was shy of our simple food on your visits. Later I have learned that simplicity is also a part of diversity in the kitchens of the world. There is no need to compare which is better: a soloist with a background or the entire symphony orchestra :)

I feel I owe much to you, and have learned a lot from you. The big difference between our cultures has not in any way troubled, but only enriched our lives. I hope we have been able to give you back something to show our respect for you. Even if we may like different things, almost all our values are common, like respecting other people, responsibility, diligence, and honesty. Your important mission has been to increase the respect and equality of Thai women. It has always been important to you to represent your country and increase the consciousness of Thai culture in Finland. The people here unfortunately tend to have a stereotypical and shallow view of Thailand -as well as of many other countries around the world. Increasing the knowledge of culture, if anything, creates tolerance and supports world peace. You have acted as a cultural ambassador of your country meritoriously.

Your and Pasi's giant cultural effort was the Thai music and food festival at the Sibelius Akatemia on October 1st, 2005. I participated by promoting the event to my friends and at work, and filled a table there with friends and colleagues. It was a very good way to get to know Thai culture in many ways. All senses were pampered. Unfortunately we Finns didn't have more time or courage to participate. The event would have needed many more visitors for a financial success.

You, Porntipa, have been a tremendous example for both your children and for everybody knowing you. You are not afraid of failure, and you have the courage to fulfill your dreams. You haven't let disbelievers put you down when you have decided something. When other people contemplate, you already do and act. Your motto would be "Adversities are made to be conquered".

You weren't afraid to leave to a foreign country with a language difficult to learn. You have worked here from the very beginning, taking care of your family and setting up a business of your own. You always remember to thank Pasi as well. The word you use often, with love and tenderness, is *"family"*. By which you mean not just your own family but also your mother and your brother and sister, as well as Pasi's parents and sisters and their families. You have said that gratitude is a great resource to you.

My family is very happy and privileged having been able to know you and your family. You have brought a new dimension to our life. For that I thank you from the bottom on my heart!

Raija Marja-Aho

Bibliography and references

Thank you to the book "Thamma Banterng Lai Ruang Lao" Chuan Muan Cheun by Ajarn Phrom Vongso

"How to Win Friends and Influence People" by Dale Carnegie

Thank you to the magazines "Fah Deow Gan" and "Ahn" (tri-monthly)

Thank you for information from "Kid Hen Len Tang" by Khun Kampaka on Voice TV, Diva's Café, "Trong Pai Trong Ma" program by Asia Update, "Kor Prai Nee Ka 2" by Kampaka, "Poo Ying Khua Buak" by Kampaka.

About the Author

Porntipa Ilvesmäki is 52 years old. She is a southerner from Amphur Hat Yai, Songkhla province, and is the youngest daughter of Pratuang and Priya Jitnarong.

> Her brother is Pachai Jitnarong.
> Her sister is Pratana Pattano.
> She was born into the restaurant and tailoring business.
> She is married to a Finn called Pasi Ilvesmäki
> Her eldest son is Kittipong Jitnarong
> Her second son is Jussi Ilvesmäki
> Her youngest daughter is Jasmin Ilvesmäki.

Today, she is well-respected as a Thai cultural ambassador abroad. She has supported Thailand's joining of the ASEAN community and supported democracy in Thailand. Her interests include literature, history, politics, Thai culture, and she has a following of foreign food lovers who admire her Thai cooking. Her fruit, vegetable and soap carving have generated a large following and large queues of people have formed to wait for her carved soaps and handicrafts.

She now enters a new role as an author, bringing her knowledge and experience as a Thai woman living abroad to share through **"The Foreign In-Law"**, a source of pride and joy for the author and her family.

www.ingramcontent.com/pod-product-compliance
Lightning Source LLC
Chambersburg PA
CBHW050140170426
43197CB00011B/1909